P9-CKX-958

why writing matters

yale

university

press

new haven

and

london

nicholas

delbanco

why

writing

matters

Montrose Reg. Library Dist.
320 S. 2nd St.
Montrose, CO 81401

"Why X Matters" and the yX logo are registered trademarks of Yale University.

Copyright ©2020 by Nicholas Delbanco. All rights reserved. This book may not be reproduced, in whole or in part, including illustrations, in any form (beyond that copying permitted by Sections 107 and 108 of the U.S. Copyright Law and except by reviewers for the public press), without written permission from the publishers.

Published with assistance from the Louis Stern Memorial Fund.

Yale University Press books may be purchased in quantity for educational, business, or promotional use. For information, please e-mail sales.press@yale.edu (U.S. office) or sales@yaleup.co.uk (U.K. office).

Set in Adobe Garamond types by IDS Infotech Ltd. Printed in the United States of America.

Library of Congress Control Number: 2019945866
ISBN 978-0-300-24597-4 (hardcover : alk. paper)

A catalogue record for this book is available from the British Library.

This paper meets the requirements for ANSI/NISO Z39.48-1992 (Permanence of Paper).

10 9 8 7 6 5 4 3 2 1

also by nicholas delbanco

For Daniel Herwitz
And Daniel Okrent
Close friends and close readers, both.

contents

author's note

This short book has been long a'borning. It was engendered by my column in the *New York Times* "Writers on Writing" series called "From Echoes Emerge Original Voices" (June 21, 1999), which described a course I was then teaching called "Strategies in Prose." The fifth chapter here reprints a version of that syllabus. That "strategy" in turn produced "In Praise of Imitation," an article in *Harper's Magazine* as long ago as July 2002. It further served as a basis for the introductory material to a textbook titled *The Sincerest Form: Writing Fiction by Imitation* (McGraw-Hill, 2003). The opening passage of Chapter 2 repeats some of the argument of *The Sincerest Form;* it has been my hobbyhorse for years.

I first taught "Strategies in Prose" at Bennington College in the early 1980s, then variations on that theme at Columbia University and the University of Michigan in the decades since. By now I've preached this particular gospel to hundreds of undergraduate and graduate students, many of whom have gone on to successful careers as writers and some of whom have taught the course in their respective institutions. In 2015—just short of half a century after my first foray into the classroom—I retired with the jaw-cracking title of Robert Frost Distinguished University Professor of English Language and Literature, and Professor Emeritus of English Language and Literature, College of Literature, Science, and the Arts at the University of Michigan. Enough's enough.

Yet the art of writing still seems to me to be grounded in an act of imitation: mimesis rules the form. It's time now to revisit the idea of reproduction and yoke it to the larger question of originality. Though I intend to concentrate on the creative mode in language, the issue feels germane as well to any discussion of music or the visual arts, not to mention our culture writ large. We value, as a culture, both the mass-produced artifact and the craftsman-like "one of a kind." The false opposition of *teacher* and *student* seems a case in point. If one ideal of democracy is full participation and "the more the merrier," there's a concomitant ideal of being singled out and standing up alone. How to reconcile that thesis and antithesis is my project here.

Excerpts from these chapters have been published in *AWP: The Writer's Chronicle* (February 2018) and my column, "Talking about Books," of *Michigan Today* at the University of Michigan. At the excellent urging of John Donatich and Sarah Miller of Yale University Press, I have expanded the topic to address the more general titular question of "why writing matters" at all. Its role is worth the pondering; its history, the recounting. To have had the occasion to do so has been, for me, a gift.

preface

Writing matters. Why? This is not a rhetorical question, and the fact we need to ask it may come as a surprise. But for reasons large and small it remains a question in contemporary culture, and one that should be answered in the pages of a book. That a book *has* pages, and that the pages contain words built out of letters, seems self-evident, a thing we take for granted—like electric light or running water or the need for heat in winter.

It was not always so. Writing is the junior sibling—the great-great-grandchild, even—of speech. Shouts and screams came first. Unnumbered eons passed before the sounds that men and women make became a sound transcribed. A murmur or a growl or pointed finger or chest-thump sufficed to beguile an intimate or to warn an enemy. Only long years later did the words *I love you,* or *Keep your distance, stranger,* take shape as articulate speech. And all of this was fleeting; before the invention of writing, spoken discourse could not last. For African griots or the Rig Veda or the epic poems of Homer, the mode of transmission was oral and subject to forgetfulness or change. We have no way of knowing how much of the language is lost.

Writing matters. Why? Although symbolic expression has been with us as a species since the dawn of what we call "recorded" time, the practice of writing is much less ancient than that of pictorial art. More than thirty thousand years ago the clan in Altamira in the north of Spain learned to decorate their rock-roof with images of bison, but the letters *b-i-s-o-n* had not as yet been shaped. Indeed, our ability to picture a *boar* or *cow* or *boat* or *crow* because of an agreed-on arrangement of letters is a gift that keeps on giving; it's imagination linked to knowledge and a central mode of growth. It's one of the ways we preserve our shared culture, a signal to the future and a record of the past.

So somewhere in some distant place and time some someone made a mark on stone or wood or ice or clay or sand and somebody else understood it and the process of writing began. It's been with us ever since. We may "read" the tides or clouds or tracks of game for what they say of water or weather or the likelihood of food. A pattern of hooves or alignment of rocks may tell the experienced hunter which way to look for sustenance or shelter, but a sign that reads "McDonald's" or "Welcome to Kansas City" requires, of its witness, a different kind of skill. By now the gift of literacy is one we have come to rely on and, as a species, prize. The elders of the tribe still school their children carefully in *A*, then *B*, then *C* . . .

Writing and reading are, of course, two sides of the same coin. The latter depends on the former; the former makes no difference where the latter ability does not exist. Those words describing its absence—*illiterate, analphabetic, abecedarian*—are terms of pity if not shame. Conjoined, however, the two skills herald learning, and it's no accident that burned or banned books assault the very notion of civilization itself. To hold an object in one's hand that forms a collection of symbols in recognized sequence, then to read those lines aloud or in attentive silence is—and has been long acknowledged as—a mark of education. It's one of the ways we distinguish ourselves from animals and plants. To paraphrase Descartes (or offer up a variation on his theme), "I write, therefore I am."

Like the carpenter or blacksmith, that member of a clan who could decipher writing had a particular function and was set apart. In the inner temple or the council house, the one who could read signs and portents was one who commanded respect. And ownership or stewardship of other people's written discourse was seen as doubly special, a mark of high-born status. To possess a text and be empowered to read it was, early on, a sign of privilege, of wealth and social standing. The "personal library" used to belong only to the chosen few: scholars or clerics or kings.

Now everyone who's anyone has—or is supposed to have—access to a book. What you hold here in your hand is neither a vanishing species nor a threatened rarity; though we may lament the loss of widespread bookishness, there are more volumes now in print and for sale than ever in our history before. And though the system of transcription may have altered—moving from hieroglyph to emoji, from an illuminated *Book of Hours* to a near-instantaneous tweet—the intention of it stays the same: language composed to be looked at and by its witness absorbed. This isn't a function of whether we hold in our palm a book or digitally transmitted pixels; what counts are the words in prearranged sequence, the paragraphs and ideas . . .

Further, one of writing's crucial components is, in effect, that of outreach; it permits communication with someone far away or from another time. You don't have to know a person "in person" to benefit from their experience, or to take comfort from a page. A distant stranger or as-yet-unborn reader can profit from instruction, once it's written down. This is why, perhaps, the burning of the library in Alexandria (in 48 BCE) remains a scar in our collective consciousness and on the body politic; it heralded collapse. Five centuries thereafter, the so-called Dark Ages went dark in part because the few remaining books were hidden away, unavailable, and the "renaissance" or rebirth of European civilization came about in part because old texts were rediscovered and brought again to light.

Although oral traditions are central to the preservation of culture, it's also true that the oral tradition has been supplanted by print. Where once we passed on knowledge by reciting it, then memorizing what was said, we now have the additional resource of language in writing preserved. If—to take only a single example— our Constitution were a verbal agreement, and not set down on paper, it would have small present claim on our judiciary. Hammurabi's code (a codex in the Akkadian tongue inscribed in cuneiform for the sixth Babylonian king nearly four thousand years ago) established the kingdom-wide value of goods and penalties for bad behavior because it was marked on a 7.5-foot stone stele. The

Dead Sea Scrolls inform us of the mores of those who read them, just as they informed their readers of a system of belief. When Moses came down from the mountain with the Ten Commandments, they were—or so the story goes—incised on a tablet; when Martin Luther objected to aspects of Catholic practice, he put those objections in writing and nailed them to the Wittenberg church doors.

The sacred scrolls and secret texts of almost every culture share the fact of being written, no matter with which symbols or in which alphabet. To nullify an oath or treaty is harder once the treaty or oath has been signed. When a word has been transcribed on paper or parchment or marble or slate, it lays claim to consequence. Written language has a gravitas only rarely accorded to speech.

These are sweeping assertions, brave claims. They need some spelling out. This book will be an effort to demonstrate, in writing, why writing does and should matter. I have spent my life engaged by it, as a writer of fiction and nonfiction. There are other forms of expression, of course (poetry, playwriting, history, biography, autobiography, etc.) and I have tried my hand at each, but my focus here will be on the genre of prose fiction. It's the creative mode with which I'm most familiar and for which my heartbeat beats.

This is not, in the strict sense, a scholarly text. A "Note on Sources" ends the book, but most of my citations are part of common parlance and readily available. Other authors have weighed in elegantly and extensively on the history of language, the evolution of writing, the acquisition of reading, on vision and revision, the way words are coined or change. So though I look at the tradition, I do so only glancingly; I'm more concerned with where we find ourselves at the present moment than with where we've been.

Nor will this book be predictive; we cannot know for certain what the digital revolution entails. In 1455, the German blacksmith, goldsmith, printer, and publisher Johannes Gutenberg engendered (or at any rate facilitated) an enormous change in Western culture with his deployment of movable type and what became known as the Gutenberg Bible. Thereafter, copies could be multiple, and the "volume" of writing increased. But no matter how prescient, the printer could neither have guessed at nor imagined the desktop 3-D version of his printing press, a commonplace today. So we at the birth (or at most the infancy) of the computer age cannot predict what will come next; suffice it to say that the blog and tweet and viral posting and Snapchat and Kindle have altered the nature of language transmission as did Gutenberg before.

We live in the forest and can see only the trees.

Certain trees, however, reward close scrutiny. In the chapters that follow I plan to examine aspects of teaching and being a student, of several seminal texts in our culture, of imitation, originality, and the creative process writ both small and large. The "root" of writing is deep-buried and must be preserved. To continue with if not belabor the comparison, there are some trees now almost altogether extinct in America—the chestnut, the Dutch elm—that once were omnipresent. Yet the green canopy survives and, in some places, thrives.

Why Writing Matters, therefore, is intended both as explanation and an exhortation; the next time you pick up a pencil or pen—or turn on your cellphone or iPad—remember you join in a long-standing practice and a time-honored tradition. It will help to know a little more about the terms of that tradition—what the Palmer Method consists of, for example, and why it lost its currency, or what we mean when we "subscribe" to an idea or magazine or "underwrite" a loan. That "mark on stone or wood or ice or clay or sand" became a mark on paper, and the word "paper" derives from papyrus, a tall aquatic plant of the sedge family that grows in the Nile Valley. When pressed and rolled and written upon, it gave us this enduring thing: spoken language transcribed, a *lingua,* a tongue. And by another alchemy, that tongue when written down became the writer's voice.

why writing matters

Teachers

Two of my models are *Teacher,* by Sylvia Ashton Warner (1963) and a collection of talks by Eudora Welty called *One Writer's Beginnings* (1984). Both are splendid books and both of them committed to advance by indirection; they wind their way from personal experience to general assertion and the overarching issue: how does one study, how teach? Pedagogy is their subject: learning to read and to write. The first person enters in, as it must in any autobiographical account, but in neither instance does the writer insist on stage center. I hope, in the pages that follow, to follow where they led.

A first emblem of instruction takes place when I was fourteen. (There are other and previous ones, of course, but childhood memories or the acquisition of and devotion to language are not my present point.) In the Fieldston School, in Riverdale, New York, our ninth-grade teacher was a man by the name of Dean Morse. My image of him is clear but blurred: youngish, wearing glasses and a Harris Tweed jacket and brown polished shoes. Though to my adolescent eyes he seemed august and well-established, I imagine he was not yet thirty-five. Most of the faculty at Fieldston had been teaching there for years, and Mr. Morse was a relative stranger; I don't think he lasted all that long and don't know what became of him or if he remained in the "trade." I was his student in the sense that there were twenty of us in the room, jockeying for position and hoping turn by turn to earn or escape his attention.

All this happened more than sixty years ago. But I remember, vividly, a conversation we once had.

The Scarlet Pimpernel, by Baroness Orczy, was published in 1905. A best-seller of the period, set in the brutal aftermath of the French Revolution, it compelled my youthful admiration. So did the 1934 movie version starring Leslie Howard and Merle Oberon. A kind of precursor of Clark Kent and Superman, the Pimpernel was a seemingly vacuous English nobleman who in fact worked as the daring secret rescuer of blameless French folk in distress. His indolence was a disguise, his heroism real. His wife thought him superficial; there were romantic depths. As a boy, I dreamed of great adventure, and I'd pop up behind the couch in my parents' living room, or emerge from behind a half-closed door, to declaim:

They seek him here, they seek him there
Those Frenchies seek him everywhere.
Is he in heaven or is he in hell?
That damned elusive Pimpernel.

I loved the book. At semester's end, a group of us—school-supervised—went on a camping trip to Lake Saranac in upstate New York. Paddling inexpertly in the constant rain, we yawed our way from cove to cove and set up camp in a series of lean-tos; Mr. Morse served as our no-doubt reluctant chaperone. That night, around the campfire—after we'd eaten the near-raw hamburgers and burned hotdogs and scorched buns and washed them down with lukewarm Coca-Cola—I told our group of the Pimpernel's brilliance and quoted my quatrain. "They seek him here, they seek him there . . ."

"It's a great novel," I said. Our teacher disagreed. I went on and on, or so it seems in memory, perorating on the excellence of Orczy's text, until finally he took off his glasses and, wiping them, said, "Read it again."

That summer I did, and he was right. *The Scarlet Pimpernel* embodies the very essence of escapist fiction; it's a bodice-ripper; it candy-coats reality; it's full of coincidence and unearned attitude and empurpled prose. There are, of course, certain books that appeal to the young and the mature reader equally—think of the work of Lewis Carroll, Charles Dickens, or Mark Twain. There's much entertainment value in "the Pimpernel"; it's a perennial crowd pleaser, with its swordplay and narrow escapes. (Witness the more recent movies and television serial and Broadway show of that title; an audience still seeks "him everywhere" more than a century after the dandy's fictive birth.) That I dislike the novel now should not gainsay that once I found it fine.

But my teacher's soft impeachment has stayed with me through all the decades since; it was one of my first lessons in the art of reading and, by extension, writing. Whether or not he's still alive to register my thanks, Mr. Morse deserves them; the distance between the eleven-year-old who first applauded Orczy's work, and the fourteen-year-old who learned to dismiss it is the distance, in effect, between the unlettered and instructed reader. *Read it again!*

In twelfth grade—Fieldston called it the "sixth form"—I studied literature with a senior member of the faculty, Elbert Lenrow. His was an established reputation, and we knew we were lucky to be in the room where Mr. Lenrow taught his fabled class. The course was a survey of sorts, and an ambitious one; we read selections of Greek tragedy and comedy, the *Odyssey* and *Iliad,* the *Aeneid,* Chaucer, Dante, Shakespeare, Goethe's *Faust.* It would take a goodly while in college before I encountered a text to which I had not been at least briefly introduced in high school, and Mr. Lenrow's aesthetic was a discriminating one.

He was, I learned later, a balletomane and opera buff, one of those bachelors of independent means who taught not for the paycheck but for the reward of it, and he managed to bring Michel de Montaigne and John Stuart Mill and Samuel Taylor Coleridge to life. We read Albert Camus and Ernest Hemingway also, but his heart was in the classics, and for the bulk of a wide-ranging year he lectured on "old" books. Mr. Lenrow was bigstomached, sparse-haired, and like Mr. Morse wore glasses—often as not on the bridge of his nose or perched athwart his forehead while he peered around the room. We students sat at facing tables, seminar-style, waiting to respond to his passage-specific queries. He was exigent, impatient, and he could be brusque. In retrospect it's clear, however, that he gave us the gift of attention, suggesting in his seriousness that we could be serious too.

Our teacher sweated easily, and I can picture still the half-moons at the armpits of his shirts. They were expensive shirts. He asked us to write sonnets and Socratic dialogues; he made us read aloud from masterworks as well as the apprentice efforts we clumsily composed. Several faculty at Fieldston wrote and published poetry or short stories; his was an unswerving devotion to the work of others. Whether we were reading *Beowulf* or "The Rhyme of the Ancient Mariner" or "Dover Beach," he brought the texts to life. I was impressed by each of my teachers of English, but Elbert Lenrow stood unchallenged as and at "the head of the class."

This was ratified, for me, in 1966. At the august age of twenty-three, I applied for a faculty position at Bennington College. The novelist Bernard Malamud was taking a leave of absence, and in my youthful arrogance I believed I could replace him. Astonishingly, the members of the Department of Language and Literature agreed I should be interviewed, and in a snowstorm I arrived in the small town of North Bennington, Vermont. It was my first such academic encounter; I did not know what to expect.

We met in the house of Stanley Edgar Hyman, the Department "Secretary"—a post that rotated annually, since the college did not believe in department chairs, and no one wanted the job. Six or seven faculty trudged to his door, complaining about the weather and congratulating each other on having dug out from the storm. Bennington had a non-resident term, mid-winter, and only a rump caucus of the department attended; Malamud himself was not in town. It was clear as clear could be that the decision as to hiring lay principally in the hands of the poet Howard Nemerov.

Aristocratic yet seedy, gimlet-eyed yet withdrawn, this heir to a Fifth Avenue furrier's fortune and brother to Diane Arbus did not suffer fools gladly. Too, he thought most he encountered were fools. He had recently served as poet laureate consultant to the Library of Congress; in 1988 he would do so again. Nemerov was unimpressed by my credentials—an undergraduate degree from Harvard, a graduate degree from Columbia, a first novel soon to appear. He stared out the window, sighing; he poured himself a second glass of scotch. Others in the room asked questions; I bumbled and stumbled my way through the interview while the afternoon wore on. Then, almost as an afterthought, the poet asked where I went to high school.

I said, "Fieldston." He had too. He asked if I had ever studied with Elbert Lenrow; I said, "Yes." For the first time fixing his gaze on me, Nemerov asked what I thought of the course. By then I had despaired of gaining favorable attention or of being hired, and so I told the truth: "Best damn class I ever took."

"No further questions," said the soon-to-be-anointed winner of the Pulitzer Prize and Bollingen Prize for poetry. He donned his snow boots and muffler and gloves and walked out of the house. I had passed the test.

I'm aware that all this smacks of "the old boy's club" and preferential treatment and would no doubt not happen today. But there was a snowstorm and remedial whiskey and mine was a replacement appointment, not a full-fledged faculty search. Too, something in my answer did trigger Nemerov's approval, or at least his gambler's guess that I had been well trained. I had known enough to know I had had a great teacher; he could trust me for the rest.

"I'm going to begin by telling you I hear voices." So starts a lecture given in April 1991 at the George Edward Woodberry Poetry Room in Lamont Library, Harvard. It was offered by my old— then still vigorous—professor William Alfred, and I can quote it now because his voice has been preserved by an admiring cadre of students who produced a memorial CD. Stentorian if scratchily, the poet speaks. His "Keen for Bridget Kelly" includes the phrase, "I am disgusted by the inadequacy of tears, the mourner's armband," and ends with the elegiac, "It is amazing you should come to die. What in Christ's name is there to say but this?"

William Alfred (1922–1999) was an iconic figure to those fortunate enough to study with him. I did so as an undergraduate at Harvard in a large lecture course on the History of Drama, then a smaller set of courses on the Anglo-Saxon language and alliterative patterns from which our poetry is in important part derived. He became my informal tutor in "the writers' trade," an inspirational figure for me and many other students in the 1960s, as well as the decades beyond. Seamlessly—or so it seemed—he merged a commitment to scholarship with a readiness to act as father-confessor to those who sought him out. His infectious love of language, his learning worn lightly and self-deprecating humor, were, it seemed to us, exemplary: we wanted to know what he knew.

A poet and playwright—most notably for *Hogan's Goat* (which, not incidentally, starred a young Faye Dunaway)—William Alfred stood with one foot in the academy and one in the professional world. Robert Lowell and Elizabeth Bishop counted themselves his friends. So did the street people of Cambridge, whom he would daily bless. A fervent Catholic, he brought the Greek playwrights and Henrik Ibsen to life, yet was also au courant with the latest doings on Broadway. To be invited to his house or join him for a campus walk was to feel empowered; to hear him talk of childhood in Brooklyn or service in the army was to enlarge one's horizon. His unfailingly generous spirit, his sweet concern for the plaints and ambitions of students, his selfless dedication to the enterprise of teaching, were and are a model for unnumbered acolytes. I count myself among them. Like Dean Morse and Elbert Lenrow, he gave us the gift of attention; in William Alfred's company there was never a trace of impatience, and always he contrived to make those who joined him at table feel welcome. I have not heard his living voice for decades yet it continues to sound in my ears: a clarion call.

All this has been occasioned by an email I today received from a student (who shall remain nameless, and in truth I didn't remember her name) to whom I once was generous in 1972. Her claim—no doubt hyperbolic—is that my encouragement sustained her through almost fifty years in the pre-publication wilderness. Her soon-to-be-published first book, she wrote, owes much to my help way back when. This sort of recognition delights an old professor, but I refer to it because it seems to me emblematic of the teacher-student relation when successful; we carry—every one of us—some memory of something said in class or private that made a *difference* once. William Alfred, were he still alive, would feel just as surprised if not embarrassed by the paean of praise in these first three paragraphs as is his student by his own student's letter of thanks. To learn or read long after the fact that something you once said or wrote retains enduring currency is to feel rewarded. There's a "strange comfort afforded by the profession"—the title of a short story by Malcolm Lowry— and when we acknowledge indebtedness we join a long line of adepts who once received instruction at a master's feet. Then, in that master's honor, we try to do the same.

When talking of contemporary poets, William Alfred spoke of "that terrible failure of confidence which comes when you see something new." In his "Keen for Bridget Kelly" he memorializes a figure long gone, but she has not "come to die" because the language lives.

In the early 1960s, Harvard College tolerated the practice of creative writing but did not construe it a legitimate course of study. I majored in another discipline and only toward the end of my time there took a writing course. My teacher was Mr.—not *Professor*—Theodore Morrison, a wiry man with a shock of white hair and map of New England inscribed on his face. He carried a green bookbag and rode a bicycle to class in all sorts of weather; he told me he didn't mind winter but disliked mud season, the spring. When not residing in Cambridge, he lived in Ripton, Vermont, a village in the hills above Middlebury where the Breadloaf Writers' Conference takes place (and for which he served as director from 1932 to 1955).

He was, it turned out, a close associate of Robert Frost's, whose private secretary was Kathleen Morrison, "Ted's" wife. He published several novels and books of poetry and a critical study of Chaucer; his friends included such literary luminaries as Bernard de Voto and Wallace Stegner, but he was a modest man and not given to name-dropping. In class, he was (to use a later formulation) "laid back" and largely non-directive, yet he scrutinized our prose and poetry effusions with close care.

Back then I was beginning what would become my first book. I describe this at brief length in the ensuing pages (in the passage on John Updike) but in the fall of senior year I was working on *The Martlet's Tale* and trying on prose styles for size. The novel takes place in Greece, on the island of Rhodes. It was lyrical in the extreme. I wrote a rhapsodic passage in which I celebrated village life—the fishermen returned to shore after a long day of work on the water, and dragging their hand-built caïques up the beach to safety on the shingle and emptying their holds of smelt and sea urchins and fish for purchase and spreading out their nets to dry and building a fire with which to roast a portion of the catch and drinking ouzo and retsina wine and tuning and plucking their bouzoukis while they serenaded the countless stars above, the moon rising, the smoke rising, the song rising, their women beside them on blankets joining in the chorus and finally, as midnight drew nigh, taking their loved ones back to the huts beneath low-hanging olive trees where they, limbs entwined, embracing, fell together into their small little beds . . .

Mr. Morrison was kind. He praised the scene, the detailing, the romantic flair of it. I preened. And then he said, "I only have one question. Nick, do the beds need to be both small *and* little?"

At which point my whole verbal house of cards collapsed. I had been, I recognized, as enthralled by my descriptive prose as once, no doubt, was the Baroness Orczy, and with the same rose-colored, not to say purple, results. All these decades later, when I write "small" and "little" in an adjacent phrase, I cringe as when I learned from Theodore Morrison that less is decidedly more.

In his old age, he withdrew to Amherst, Massachusetts. He would die at eighty-seven, in 1988. Near the beginning of that decade, *Harvard Magazine* published a profile of Morrison in retirement, where—when asked if he had any regrets—he suggested he might have better spent his time producing his own creative work than enabling that of others. I was moved; I wrote him, declaring I was certain I was not alone in having profited from his instructor's generosity. I had in fact dedicated an early novel "To Theodore Morrison" and continued, I wrote, to learn from his example.

Almost by return mail, he answered, saying that he'd followed my career, was pleased by it: the handwriting small but legible, firm and unchanged, filling the page. In gratitude I wrote him back and enclosed a copy of my most recent book, a collection of short stories called *About My Table*. Again, with dizzying promptness, he responded: He admired story B, he liked story A well enough, if he understood what I was getting at in story C, it might have been useful to deploy a third-person narrative; he did not care for story D. He applauded the second paragraph of page 43, he disagreed with my choice of adjectives on page 179. And so on and so forth.

I imagine he must have been lonely and grateful for something to do. Nor can I pretend I agreed with all his critiques. But the care he'd lavished on his letter was nothing short of inspirational. Once a teacher always a teacher: it's a hard habit to break.

What follows are three memories of three major authors who influenced me greatly, though each in different ways. I'm aware that my models all are male—less surprising, perhaps, in the time of which I write than would be the case in the academy today. And there are many women who became close colleagues, from whose instruction I have profited in the world of words. But it's the flat fact of my education that the seven figures who inhabit this chapter on teaching each and all are men.

The first—John Updike—taught me what a master-disciple relation entails; the second—John Gardner—taught me about colleagueship; the third—James Baldwin—exemplified what open-handed generosity can mean. If I had to reduce their teachings to a single statement, I learned from the first about an intensity of attention to language, from the second about unswerving devotion to craft. From the third I learned that prose, no matter how carefully composed or revised, must stand in the service of faith: a faith that writing, in times of trouble, might count.

Each of these appreciations has been previously published. The most recent incarnation of my memory of Updike appeared in *John Updike Remembered: Friends, Family and Colleagues Reflect on the Writer and the Man,* edited by Jack A. De Bellis (2017); the first memory of Gardner comes from my Editor's Introduction to his posthumously published *Stillness and Shadows, Two Novels by John Gardner* (1986); and my passage on James Baldwin is in *Running in Place: Scenes from the South of France* (1989). There is of course—in each of the portraits—much more and else to say. But, beyond slight emendation, I see no reason to alter the wording of these tributes and reprint them here.

I have been the full-fledged student of a writer only once. John Updike was, I think, one of the most literate and able critics of our time. His breadth of reading, acuity of insight, and grace of expression must give most scholars pause; he would no doubt have been made welcome at any institution in any of the fifty states. But he remained at a stiff arm's remove from academe, earning his living by the pen alone. In the summer of 1962, however, his resolution wavered and he agreed to teach—at Harvard Summer School. I wanted to remain in Cambridge and therefore applied for the course. It was an offhand decision; I barely had heard of his name. When he accepted me into his fiction workshop, it would have been ungrateful to drop out.

In retrospect, I see more clearly how lucky and right was that choice. The first word I wrote for Updike was the first of my first novel. Like any self-respecting undergraduate, I intended to be either a poet, folk singer, or movie star. I considered "prose" and "prosaic" to be cognate terms. (They are, admittedly, but I know something more by now about the other three professions and would not trade.) The young man's fancy is poetic, and his models are Rimbaud or Keats. Mine were, at any rate; my first compositions were suicide notes. But I was signed up for a writing workshop with no idea of what to write and not much time to decide. The day of that decision is vivid to me still.

A friend and I were strolling around a lake in Wellesley; we'd been reading for final exams. I heard him out as to his future; then he had to listen to me. I had tried my hand already at the shorter stuff, I said; I was going to write a novel. That was what a summer should consist of—something ambitious, no piddling little enterprise like Chekhov's but something on the scale of, let's say, *Moby-Dick*.

Yet before I wrote my masterpiece I had to plan it out. What do first novels consist of, I asked—then answered, nodding sagely at a red-haired girl in a bikini emerging from the lake. First novels by men are either the myth of Narcissus or the parable of the Prodigal Son—but generally inadvertent. Their authors do not understand they fit an ancient mold. I already knew enough about Narcissus, I confessed, and therefore would elect the latter; I'd rewrite the parable. The difference was that my revision would be conscious, whereas most young novelists fail to see themselves in sufficiently explicit mythic terms.

That was not my problem, but there were problems to solve. I knew nothing about the landscape of the Bible, for instance, and should find a substitute. My friend lit a cigarette; we considered.

It happened that I'd been to Greece the previous summer and traveled wide-eyed for weeks. I would replace one location with the other. The parable has three component parts: the son leaves home, spends time away, and returns. My novel too would have three components, with Rhodes and Athens as its locales. My Greek protagonist would go from the island to city and, as in the parable, "eat up his substance with whores."

The girl in the bikini trailed drops of water where she walked; she shook her long hair free. I instructed my friend that *hetarae* in Athens had "Follow Me" incised backward on their sandals, so that they could print directions in the dust. She rounded a bend in the path. The question of contemporancity engaged me for three minutes. I knew enough about modern-day Greece to fake it, possibly, but knew I'd never know enough about the ways of antique Attica; the sign on the prostitute's sandal exhausted my store of lore. It would take less research to update the parable. So there, within ten minutes, I had it: a contemporary version of the tale of the Prodigal Son that followed the text faithfully and yet took place in Greece. The rest was an issue of filling in blanks; I started to, next week.

I have told this tongue-in-cheek, but it is nonetheless true. The epigraph of *The Martlet's Tale* is the first line of the parable; the great original is buried in my version, phrase by phrase. I revised the novel many times and by the time I'd finished was no longer a beginner. Looking back I'm astonished, however; it all fell so neatly in place. The editor at J. B. Lippincott ushered me into his office and agreed to bring out the book. "You're a very fortunate young man," he said, but I thought his politeness routine. I took success for granted when it came. My photograph in magazines seemed merely an occasion for judging the likeness; a long and flattering review in the *New York Times* on publication day was no more than an author expected; I ate expensive lunches with the cheerful certainty that someone else would pay.

In some degree, moreover, this very blindness worked to my advantage. I had been accustomed to a schoolboy's notion of success. I would have dealt with failure far less equably. Had Updike not encouraged me, I cannot say for certain if I would have persevered; there were many wind-scraps in the wind, and I followed the favoring breeze. Harvard does prepare you for the world in this one crucial way: if you succeed within its walls, you assume that you will when outside. When I handed in *The Martlet's Tale*'s first chapter, and my professor's reaction was praise, I concluded that the rest must follow as the night does day. I suppose I stood out in his class. I certainly tried to; his wary approval meant much. I wrote a second chapter and was hooked.

The hook went deep. Through later years and decades, he remained my model. His was the opinion I most valued, the endorsement I most sought. We saw each other frequently to start with, less frequently as time went on and I moved away from Vermont. The last encounter was by happy accident, at an exhibition in Manhattan we both were walking through. I'd lunched with John not long before, at a pre-arranged meeting in Boston, but this felt somehow more important because unscheduled: the chance to look at art with him and see, from a shared vantage, what he saw.

As always he instructed me: the context he established, the minutiae he observed, the things he was aware of that I would have failed to register. Each time we paused to focus (on photographs of post-Katrina New Orleans, in the Metropolitan Museum of Art), he pointed out something I might not have noticed, or surely not so rapidly and surely not so well. *Just Looking* and *Still Looking,* his collections of art criticism, attest to his alertness and wide-ranging eye.

Once I drove him on a road near Bennington I'd driven over often—past a house I passed on an almost daily basis and that to my certain knowledge he had never seen before. John made a remark about the "shuddering roof line" of the ancient structure, and then the way the shutters were hung, and I realized to my respectful shame that he in one assessing glance had captured what in hundreds of trips I myself had failed to see. Henry James's injunction—"Try to be one of those on whom nothing is lost"— fit Updike perfectly; nothing escaped his attention.

So my relation to him, always, was that of admiring acolyte— and though in later years I did muster reservations and oppositional opinions, he was my master, first and last. He was, I think, not sorry to claim me as his student, and I was always proud to claim that as my role. There are letters exchanged, books signed and sent, postcards and photographs shared. His archive at Harvard's Houghton Library is vast, and I play only a modest part in it, but one of his last letters to me is a text I cherish and reprinted in my book on elder artists: *Lastingness: The Art of Old Age* (2011). In it Updike resoundingly writes: "Aesthetic flourishes fade and wrinkle, though they may get attention when new. A blunt sincerity outlasts finely honed irony, I would think."

His work was full of "aesthetic flourishes" and "finely honed irony"; in the end there was "a blunt sincerity" as well. R.I.P.

The cover illustration of John Gardner's collection of short stories, *The Art of Living*, shows a motorcyclist racing at the reader, straight ahead. His jacket is black leather, as was John's, and his expression is grim. It is as though he drives *In the Suicide Mountains*—another of the author's titles—prepared to take the leap described on the final page of *Grendel;* there are fierce night rides throughout his work, and creatures everywhere at risk.

John Champlain Gardner, Jr., died of injuries sustained in a motorcycle accident on Tuesday, September 14, 1982. The afternoon was balmy, bright; the roads were dry. He was an experienced driver, a few miles from home; he swerved—to avoid another vehicle, perhaps?—and fell. John was forever trying to explain himself, but death is inexplicable; the coroner's report describes result, not cause. It is clear he was trying to make it, fighting to survive. We never will know what he saw while he fell, or felt when the handlebar dealt him its mortal gut punch.

He maintained, repeatedly, that he had no fear of death; he wanted the rider of *The Art of Living* to appear playful, not fierce. On September 16, two days after the accident, my wife and I received a letter from him full of future plans. He was to marry a third time on the weekend of what became his funeral; he was immersed in a translation of *Gilgamesh*—"Fine pome!"; he sounded, as always, vividly alive.

John seemed somehow to have been born with a quicker ratio to the passage of time than the rest of us. He worked with a headlong, hurtling rush—at times, twenty hours a day. Each new home for him, I think, was absolutely home; each new set of friends was old and dear and gifted; his moderation was our excess and his excess brooked no containment. It's not so much a question of the forced march and furious pace, as if he knew he might die young and wanted to waste or miss nothing. Rather, it was as if he decided that artistic matters demanded all the patient seriousness he had. He had no attention left to squander on sleep or table manners or the IRS . . .

Others knew him longer and more intimately. I offer this account of friendship in the knowledge it was representative; many shared in the general loss. We met on Tuesday, April 16, 1974. I was teaching at Bennington College, and he was on a reading tour; he and his wife, Joan, arrived for dinner at our house.

My first impression of Gardner remains: a rotund, pipe-smoking man, with a high-pitched voice and rapid rate of utterance, pontificating splendidly and as if by rote. His eyes were red-rimmed, his white hair lank; he made his entry two hours late. It was not his fault, in fact; it was Albany airport's, and the fog's. But somehow, in the ensuing years, there would always be some such disruption: a car would fail to start or end up in a ditch, a snowstorm would come out of nowhere, a wallet would be misplaced. Joan Gardner wore expensive clothing and fistfuls of jewelry; the novelist wore blue jeans and a cracked black leather vest. He emptied a near-full quart of vodka before he sat to eat.

I saw him often in such situations later; they are hard to avoid. Fame brings a constant, admiring assault, a request from strangers to be brilliant or outrageous or at least informed. It wears one down and forces one to substitute a mask for face; sooner or later, they fuse. This is doubly a danger for the writer, since privacy is the sine qua non of his work and he has had no training in the actor's life.

By midnight I had dropped my guard; by two o'clock he had too. Elena, my wife—eight months pregnant—went to sleep. Since I had to teach next morning, I tried to call a halt; I had to prepare for my class.

Nonsense, said John, we'd have another bottle and he'd help me through the morning session—what was it on, by the way? "Virginia Woolf," I said, and construed his nodding to mean knowledge of her work. So we talked till four or five and met again at ten o'clock; I weaved my way to class.

In the event I did most of the teaching. Perhaps I knew more about Virginia Woolf; certainly I felt more responsible to the students than did their visitor. I lectured with a panicky inventiveness, stopping only for questions or breath. The session went well; I knew that. But Gardner assured me, with what I later came to recognize as characteristic hyperbole, that it was the best talk he'd ever attended—at least, on any author after Malory. He knew something more than I did, maybe, about Apollonius of Rhodes, but my talk took the modern-day cake. I was gratified, of course, and all the more so when his wife said he repeated the praise to her later; we had become "fast friends." The next night, after his reading, I asked if he wanted a job.

I was in the position to hire him but did not believe he'd accept. It was more an offhand courtesy, a variety of "If you'd ever care to come back through . . ." To my surprise he said yes. He was tired of his present appointment, possibly; his family hoped to move east. At the end of *Stillness*—a posthumously published autobiographical novel—he records the accidental-seeming sequence that brought him to Vermont. We were in his motel room; he was changing shirts. This completes my introductory image: a white-fleshed, big-bellied man with his pants' legs rolled up, his pipe smoking on the coverlet, and papers all over the bed. Students clustered at the motel entrance, waiting to whisk him away. The last thing that he handed me was a drawing of himself as gnome, peeping out from bushes with the block-letter legend, "Should Nicholas require John Gardner, he can be reached at . . ." his number and address in Illinois. I did require him, and he could be reached.

For three years thereafter, we saw each other continually. His presence was a gift. He ballyhooed my work in public and berated it in private. Day in, week out, we wrangled over prose. There was nothing polite or distanced about his sense of collegueship; if he hated a line he said so, and if he hated a character he said so all the more loudly. At this remove it's hard to remember what we discussed at such length: profluence, *energeia,* walnut trees. I spent three days hunting through graveyards and telephone books in order to prove that Sherbrooke with an *e*—the surname of a character in the novel I was writing—would be more likely than Sherbrook without. He came up with a whiskey bottle spelled Sherbrook; I pointed to a Sherbrooke township southeast of Montreal. We co-taught classes and founded a summer writing workshop together. Out of many memories I will here cite two.

October Light was accorded the National Book Critics Circle Award for fiction in 1976. The presentation ceremony took place in New York, and John's publishers made it an occasion. They hosted a supper party afterward, and a suite was reserved in Gardner's name at the Algonquin Hotel. He asked Elena and me to be his companions that night. He wore the dungarees we'd seen him wear all month; the two of us dressed to the nines. He was energetic, affable—but most of all, and in a way that's impossible to overstate, he was serious. Where other writers would have rested on their laurels, he was busy lobbying for his present project—an opera. He was no good at small talk, too abrupt; he was busy all night long. This helps explain his torrential outpouring those years; he did not stop. His first question to me, always, was "What are you working on?" *October Light* was finished, therefore irrelevant.

The occasion was a success. There were important and beautiful people, good speeches and fine wines. At night's end we repaired to the Algonquin, where they nearly refused him a bed. He had a typewriter and briefcase as luggage, no credit cards or cash. We somehow convinced the desk clerk that Alfred Knopf himself would foot the bill, and were escorted to the suite. There were flowers and fruit, bottles waiting on ice; we ordered brandy as well. As the bellhop left, John sat. The couch was vast. He sank in its plush lushness, and mice scrambled from his feet.

They were gone quickly; they scurried to some other section of the suite. But in that first instant I thought they emerged from his boots. We laughed. We placated Elena and informed the bellhop on his return that he should make certain hereafter to clear away the cheese. Yet the image remains and retains its first power to shock: I saw his power in the process of collapse. The telephone rang.

At home he would answer, "Hello, Gardners." That was, he explained, a way of being noncommittal; it was a large family, and you never knew which one the caller intended. It was also a way of keeping celebrity seekers at bay; you didn't have to say, "John Gardner" and could therefore always say he wasn't in.

It rang again.

He answered, "Hello, Gardner." He seemed forlorn; the brandy and Book Critics Circle Award had no power to invigorate. He was white and tired and, for all our efforts at support, alone.

Within the year, he was operated on for cancer. His first marriage had ended; his second—to a Bennington graduate, the poet L. M. Rosenberg—was in the offing, and he had moved from Vermont. They took him to Johns Hopkins Medical Center for emergency surgery; on Christmas I flew down. At dawn on Christmas Day the airports are deserted, so I had an empty, easy flight and arrived in Baltimore by nine.

He had not expected me and was watching television. His usual pallor was more pronounced still and made the sheet seem colorful. When he saw me, he blushed. It was, I teased him, the first and only time he'd been caught in the act of watching TV; James Page, the protagonist of John's *October Light,* had shot out the television screen in his house. So it would not have been pleasure but embarrassment that caused him to flush—but it was all right, I assured him, his secret addiction was safe. I blathered on like that until we felt at ease with silence; against hospital rules he lit up his pipe; all was well. I presented Christmas tokens; he complained about the trouble he was having with a paragraph; he had worked at it for three days now, but it wasn't right. The medicine tray held his IBM Selectric typewriter, and the window ledge was heaped with twenty-weight bond. (The next time I visited him at Hopkins he was sitting up in bed and busily at work—irritable, almost, at the interruption. The third time Elena came too, and we could not find him; he was in the reaches of the hospital basement, having commandeered a Xerox machine.) But that first instant when I watched him through the open door remains the image here. I knew—to see him reaching for the TV monitor and then for his pipe, turning even this cell into a work space, disorderly—he would survive.

His work will. Novelist, poet, critic, playwright, librettist, scholar, translator, fabulist: at forty-nine years old, he had the exuberance and protean energy of men not half his age. He was involved in the theater, in music, woodworking, publishing, teaching, painting: any number of pursuits and none of them casual or slapdash. His paintings were intensely seen; his boxes and furniture served. I remember dropping by his house in Bennington to find so many bookshelves fabricated in one day that I thought the pipe smoke he stood wreathed in had caused my eyes to blur. He did seem, somehow, multiple. The first musical selection of the memorial service on East Main Street in Batavia—the town in upstate New York where he was born and buried—was a cassette of John and his son Joel, performing on their French horns. They played "Amazing Grace."

More than half my life ago, I was a near neighbor of James Baldwin. We'd met in the winter of 1970, briefly, in Istanbul. I had been working on the screenplay for the film of my first novel, and the director knew Baldwin, and Baldwin was in town. We had a drink together and went to *Fortune and Men's Eyes,* a play he directed in Turkish. Not knowing Turkish, I was less than en-thralled, and the meeting did not matter much and the evening was a blur. The next year, however, my wife and I moved to the South of France as newlyweds, and we ran into Baldwin in Cannes. Standing on line at the American Express office, in what seemed like an interminable forward progress, I recognized the writer behind me. We shook hands. Then I said that the director who had introduced us would be passing through, and maybe we could get together for a meal or drink.

I was surprised, I think, by his alacrity; we went to his house the next day. Elena's daybook for our final ten days in Provence lists five such occasions: dinner at his house, at ours, at a restau-rant in Saint-Paul-de-Vence, talks and walks. He was completing *No Name in the Street;* he was planning to remain in France and would do so for years. His openhanded welcome, his insistence that we call as soon as we came back meant much, as did his cheerful certainty that we would return.

In 1973, when we settled again in the house in Provence, Baldwin treated us like long-lost friends. By then he had established a work pattern and an entourage. The writer had a chauffeur large enough to double as a bodyguard, a cook, a companion named Philippe who acted as a kind of secretary-manager, and various others whose function is less easy to describe. There would be a dancer or painter in tow—old lovers or associates from some project in the offing, or projected, or long past. They came from Italy, America, Algeria, Tunisia, Finland. Brothers and nephews passed through.

We were rarely less than six at table, and more often ten. The cook and the *femme de ménage* came and went; the men stayed on.

They treated their provider with fond deference, as if his talent must be sheltered from invasive detail, the rude importunate matters of fact. They answered the phone and the door. They sorted mail. There was an intricate hierarchy of rank, a jockeying for position that evoked nothing so much as a Provençal court—who was in favor, who out, who had known Jimmy longer or better or where, who would do the shopping or join him in Paris for the television interview or help with the book-jacket photo. He was working, again, on a novel: *If Beale Street Could Talk.*

Baldwin drank scotch. We drank wine. I have not as yet described the quality of kindness in his manner, the affection he expected and expressed. His face is widely known—that dark glare, broad nose, those large protruding eyes, the close-fitting cap of curls then starting to go white. But photographs cannot convey the mobile play of feature, the intensity of utterance, the sense he could contrive to give that attention *matters* and gesture can count. There was something theatrical in Jimmy's manner, and it grew automatic at times. He would embark on what seemed a tirade, a high-speed compilation of phrases that clearly had been phrased before, a kind of improvised lecture spun out of previous speech. He stared at you unblinkingly; you could not turn away. He wore elaborate jewelry and fingered it, talking; he smoked. He had been holding center stage for years.

You shifted in your seat. You said, "Yes, but . . ." and he raised his imperious manicured hand. Dialogue, for Baldwin, was an interrupted monologue; he would yield the platform neither willingly nor long. He could speak incisively on a book he had not read. But again and again he impressed me with his canny ranging, his alert intelligence. In the literal sense, I was no longer a student, but Baldwin remained a teacher at least as much as—his own early training—a preacher. "Understand me," he would say. "It's important you understand." And it *was* important, and in that mesmeric presence you thought you understood . . .

My pleasure in our meetings is easily explained. Here was the spokesman of his generation and color speaking directly to me. That he took my opinions seriously, that he read and respected my work, or appeared to, that he wanted us with him as often as possible—all this was flattering. When we parted late at night, Jimmy would say, "See you two tomorrow." If we came for lunch instead, he urged us to stay on for dinner; when a friend passed through Saint-Paul, he would insist we meet.

Why he wanted to spend time with us is, I think, less clear. Each friendship partakes of the reciprocal trade agreement, and I can only speculate as to Baldwin's motives in the trade. He was the most sociable of solitaries; though constantly attended and attended to, he held himself apart. He wanted to hear "news from home." Elena had worked several years in a rehabilitation agency for drug addicts in New York, whose clientele was largely black; she moved easily through his old streets. Though she was without exception the single woman in his house—and in a party of a dozen men— she was given pride of place. She sat at his right hand. They liked each other, I believe, with unfettered immediate liking; she treated him with just the right mixture of impatience and respect. They embraced each other, meaning it; they huddled in corners together. There was nothing exclusionary about his attitude to women; though surrounded by adoring boys he was also a "family man."

I mattered to him, I suppose, as a practitioner of a shared trade. He told me he was starved for the chance to talk books, for a discussion, say, of Henry James with someone who had read him. We talked the way most writers do, in a kind of shorthand and sign language. We asked each other, always, how the work had gone that day, how this paragraph was progressing, or that character and scene . . .

Jimmy's acolytes believed the process sacramental, as if behind his study door strange rituals took place. He would shut himself away at midnight and somehow produce an object to which accrued money and fame. They had little sense, I think, of how much it was costing him to keep them all in style, of the anxious private wrangling in the watches of the night. His acclaim had diminished of late, and he knew I knew it. The alchemy of which his friends were confident was less mysterious to me and therefore more compelling; he worked at continual risk. And I was moved by his intensity, his struggle with a form that had come to seem elusive. *Beale Street* is not as finely honed as *Go Tell It on the Mountain* or *Giovanni's Room.* That Baldwin had been consequential to a multitude of readers made all of this more poignant; he had made himself the benchmark to be passed.

Much of what I knew of the plight of the black American I had learned from reading him. And what sometimes seemed like paranoia could be argued as flat fact. The deaths of Malcolm X, of Medgar Evers, Martin Luther King, Bobby Kennedy, George Jackson, the named and nameless legion in what he called "the royal fellowship of death"; his own impending fiftieth birthday; the sickness of a beloved friend and mentor, the painter Beauford Delaney—all weighed heavily that winter. "This face," he'd say, and frame it with his slender glinting fingers. "Look at this crazy face."

In the early 1970s Richard Nixon reigned unchallenged. The Watergate scandal was building but the hearings had not yet begun. Each day brought more darkness to light. One litmus test for national allegiance, perhaps, has to do with political scandal; the French took corruption for granted, but we were transfixed. We rushed out for the paper and listened to the radio daily, but a "smoking gun" or upheaval in the political affairs of France could trigger no equivalent concern.

We waited like literal exiles for the summons to return. We discussed America with the fervor of the unrequited lover, curdling into scorn. We went for walks; we dawdled over drinks; we visited each other ("Hey, baby, what's up?" "Hey, darlin,' where've you *been?*") often and often those months.

Elena and I had been at his house in Saint-Paul-de-Vence two or three times in a row; it was our turn, therefore, to invite the Baldwin clan. We did so, one Thursday, for lunch. They said they would come, happily; they were seven, maybe nine. The two members of his party I remember as men passing through were a dancer called Bertrand and a publisher named Willi. The former was lean, lithe, beautiful, and black; he danced at the Folies-Bergère. The latter was mountainous, white. We had been warned about his appetite by Baldwin's cook days before: Willi was a voracious eater who had sent her to the market three times that afternoon.

Elena planned a *navarin;* we made an extra pot. A *navarin,* though simple, takes time to prepare; we started the previous day. We peeled turnips and carrots and leeks. We cubed the lamb and browned it, then fashioned the *bouquet garni*. Our landlady knocked. She was hoping we might join her tomorrow for lunch; there were people she thought we should meet. Lilo Rosenthal was eighty years old; she owned the property of which we occupied the gatehouse, and she was being generous to her youthful tenants. But we made our excuses, inviting her in; as she could see we too were preparing a meal. We would therefore be unable to join her, for we owed a friend a thank-you *navarin*. I remember not naming his name. Part of this was inverse snobbery, a distaste for glitter by association, and part the suspicion that, had Lilo known Baldwin was coming, we should have had to invite her. They would have been water and oil.

At any rate, she told us, she hoped we would take in our wash. It hung on the clothesline outside. She intended to walk by the gatehouse and let her friends take photographs; they were passionate photographers. Her friends were distinguished, she said. They were the last of the Hapsburgs and the last of the Hohenzollerns, respectively. Or perhaps they were the last of the Schleswigs and Holsteins, or collateral branches instead. In any case they were old and distinguished and would not appreciate the laundry on our line. She hoped we would ready the place.

We promised. We made the second *navarin,* brought an extra dozen bottles from the *cave,* bought three additional *boules* from the baker, and waited for Jimmy to come. He himself did not drive. He had, however, purchased a brand-new Mercedes, dark brown and substantial, just short of stretch-limousine size. His driver would be working that day, he had assured me, and he was bringing Bertrand, Daro, Philippe, Billy, Willi, and Bernard.

At the appointed hour we were ready; a car came. The day was overcast. What pulled into the parking space between our gatehouse and the villa was not Jimmy's Mercedes but an ancient gray Renault. It was followed, funereally, by a Deux Chevaux. Lilo Rosenthal appeared. Her guests emerged. They were slow and small and bent. The process of arrival took some time. The doors opened, faltered, closed. The last of the Hapsburgs and the last of the Hohenzollerns wore dark suits and carried cameras and advanced with umbrellas and canes. They shuffled off together to their hostess's house.

As soon as they were out of sight we heard another car. The deep-throated growl of gears, the high hum of power in harness, the trumpeting bravura of the horn—and Baldwin's Mercedes roared up. It spat the raked gravel; it rocked on its brakes; it fairly pirouetted in the sudden sun. Four doors flung wide in unison; our company had come!

They were dressed for the occasion, grandly. They wore boaters and foulards. Their boots gleamed. Bertrand especially was splendid; he emerged twirling his scarf and waist-sash of pink silk. He did a few dance steps and flung his hat high and extended his hands for applause. We applauded. Jimmy embraced us; we, him. The chauffeur was not happy with the switchbacks of the entry drive. "They're badly banked," he said. He had brought his lunch along and elected to stay with the car. He stood, arms folded, glowering down through the olive groves; he was Danish, thick and stolid and impervious to charm. "What a charming place," the publisher proclaimed. We piloted them in.

This was not easy; they swarmed. They raced to the crest of the meadow and walked tiptoe along the rim of the irrigating cistern that doubled as a pool. They approved the view. They clattered through our little house, exclaiming at the style of it, posing on the bedroom balcony. "Give me the simple life," they chorused. "Let's have *la vie en rose.*" Philippe had brought flowers; he garlanded Elena, Daro, Jimmy, Willi, and Bertrand. We emptied four bottles of wine by the time we settled to eat.

The *navarin* was a success. The publisher, Willi, approved. Audibly, he sighed, sitting back on the banquette and rolling up his sleeves. "Which pot's for me?" he asked. There were olives and pâté. There was much laughter, celebration, conversation, praise for the salads and bread. The dining room could barely contain us; we rolled about the table like a litter of puppies suckling, jostling, slicing sausages and cheese and fruit and cake. A shadow appeared at the window. I looked up.

Lilo Rosenthal was outside by the car. She and her four companions were inching up to the house. They had their cameras at shoulder level, focusing, and it pained them, clearly, to approach.

We must have looked, to them, like Spengler's nightmare realized: the decline of the West. The beaming black man at the center, the lithe array around him, the voluminous white man with loaves in his hands, the young hosts plying everyone with wine, the pyramid of bottles, the ruckus of festivity, the Mercedes being polished—all this was hard to focus on or frame. I could see Lilo explaining. I do not know how she explained. There was no laundry, however. They circled warily. We did not invite them in. They moved to the back of the house.

2 imitation

I have carried with me now for years the notion of writers as artisans: artists engaged in a guild. My model is that of the medieval guild, with its compelling triad of apprentice, then journeyman laborer, then Master Craftsman— this last attained after a lifetime's study and practice of the craft. That writing *is* a craft as well as art is something all accomplished authors take to be self-evident. Every professor professes it; every student studies it. Practice makes, if not perfect, a better practitioner; if we swing a baseball bat or golf club forty thousand times in order to improve our game, why not hone the skills of imitation too?

The habit begins in the cradle; we copy what we watch. That delighted codger lifting arms and clapping hands while a grandchild does the same is teaching by repeated gesture: *How big is baby? So-o-o big!* We learn by the example of others to walk and dress and brush our teeth and play tennis or the violin; it's how we learn to spell and drive and hunt and fish and swim. It's the way we first acquire language and, later, languages. *How does the cow go? Moo-Moo!* In every act of reading there's an agreement, however unspoken, that we follow where the author leads; the very act of printing books consists of repetition. And if what we study is writing, it's surely how we learn to write; all writers read all the time.

Often this process of replication is unconscious or only partly conscious. We hear a phrase and repeat it; we memorize the lines of a joke or ceremony or play. Those authors we admire have a habit of seeing, of *saying* the world, and when we lift our heads from the lines of a page we're likely to see as they saw.

In *Webster's New Collegiate Dictionary*, "imitation" is defined as follows:

> 1. An imitating; a copying. 2. That which is made or produced as a copy; an artificial likeness. 3. Properly, a literary work designed to reproduce the style or manner of another author. 4. *Biol.* Mimicry. 5. *Music.* The repetition in a voice part of the melodic theme; phrase or motive previously found in another part. Imitation is *strict* when the original theme or phrase and its repeated form are identical in intervals and note values, *free* when the repetition has some modification.

As the fourth of these brief definitions suggests, the act of mimicry is well established in nature. The coat of mountain goats and skin tint of chameleons blend in with the rock face or leaf. A mockingbird borrows its song. The human race reproduces itself, as do snow leopards and snow peas; the Human Genome Project undertakes to map that process of transmission: how and why. But this chapter deals not so much with imitation in the biological sense as in its dictionary meaning of "a copy; an artificial likeness." Though the salmon and the polar bear may inherit via instinct their patterns of behavior, those who "reproduce the style or manner of another author" must study what they do.

In music and the visual arts, "strict" or "free" repetition is common; both ear and eye acknowledge variations on a theme. We salute the work of others in a melodic arrangement or a composition structured as a predecessor painted it; this process of "quotation" is familiar. Variation inverts, reverses, modulates, or changes rhythm while remaining wedded to a musical motif; it's the very essence of improvisation in jazz. In museums all over the country there's someone bent over an easel, doing their best to reproduce what's framed and on the wall. The techniques of mimicry—and its silent partner, mime—prove crucial to the actor's craft, advancing center stage.

In most forms of performance, indeed, we take such skills for granted, and personal expressiveness may even be a mistake. The members of a dance troupe must follow their choreographer's lead, moving in trained unison, and woe betide that member of the string section of an orchestra who chooses an exotic bowing. To be singled out while joining in a chorus is to risk correction; when you march you should do so in step . . .

I'm not suggesting here that protective coloration need be drab, or that not to be noticed is best. But for many centuries and in many different cultural contexts the standard of imitation and close reproduction held sway. It was how to learn a trade. An apprentice in a studio would have mixed paint for years or cleaned the varnish rags and swept wood shavings from the floor for what must have felt like forever; only after years and years might the young artisan depart from the studio model and start to work alone. The French instrument maker J. B. Vuillaume took his pattern for violins and violoncellos unabashedly from his much-admired predecessor Antonio Stradivari. This is not forgery so much as emulation, a willing admission that others have gone this way before . . .

So why should we exempt the art of writing from, as *Webster's* describes it, "An imitating, a copying"? We've grown so committed as a culture to the ideal of originality that the author who admits to working in the mode and manner of another author will likely stand accused of being second-rate. But to imitate is not to be derivative; it's simply to admit that we derive from what was accomplished by others.

Janus is the two-faced god who gave his name to January; poised at the turning of the year, he looks both forward and back. The artist must deploy just such a doubling vision—the microscope and telescope conjoined.

❧

"Hello."

"Hell*o*."

"Good morning."

"Good morning to *you.*"

"How do you want to spend this day?"

"Oh, getting and spending."

"I've heard that before."

"Where? When?"

"Let me try to remember."

"Try to remember . . ."

"The kind of September."

"I've heard *that* before."

"This can't go on."

"It can."

"The quick brown fox jumps over the lazy dog." In adolescence I was taught this is the most efficient sentence to contain our entire alphabet. The nine words use thirty-five letters with, admittedly, some repetitions: two "h's," "r's," "t's," and "u's"; three "e's"; four "o's." *Hey presto,* we have included all twenty-six letters of the English alphabet, a pangram from "a" to "z."

But it still seems repetitive; why not reduce the number by two? The word "the" recurs in its entirety. "*A* quick brown fox jumps over the lazy dog" would incorporate only thirty-three letters and seven repeats. Or alter placement and add a comma: "Quick, a brown fox jumps over the lazy dog." Or shift the terms of engagement: "A quick brown dog jumps over the lazy fox." Or: "Lazy, a quick brown fox jumps over the dog." There are, in effect, several variations on the theme, but those who still take typing tests or align print fonts in rows have used this first formulation since time out of mind. On February 10, 1885, the *Boston Journal* cited it as "A favorite copy set by writing teachers for their pupils." Thereafter, dozens of papers and journals displayed the same thirty-five letters: "The quick brown fox jumps over the lazy dog."

I learned this in "Shop," or more precisely, in my high-school printing class. All these decades later, I can conjure up the ink we used, the wooden racks and metal fonts and turpentine-soaked rags. Painstakingly, while other students learned to cook or handle a jigsaw or potter's wheel, a group of us would set headlines for the *Fieldston News* by hand. I still can see the printing press on those late autumn afternoons, the flickering light bulbs, the stacks of paper waiting to be trimmed. I hear the soft clicking of lead set in place, the loud clank and whir of the plates. I touch and taste the smell of it: the stained blue smocks, the clatter of pulleys and pedals, the arm of the girl at my left . . .

Things change. The computer on which I compose this has a capacity that Gutenberg could not have imagined when, in the mid-1400s, he commenced to use moveable type. Today, "Project Gutenberg" allows the reader access to almost all books in the public domain, and soon enough we'll carry entire civilizations—the contents of the British Museum and the Library of Congress—in a single hand. A smart phone or Kindle provides "palm-reading" in a manner no fortune teller foretold; the printing press and linotype have gone the way of parchment and quill pens. Where they exist, they do so as specialty objects, and those who preserve and still use them are harkening back to a long-distant past.

Even in the 1950s, manual typesetting was a shopworn practice, and I was thick-fingered, fat-thumbed. It would take me hours to produce a page. But there was palpable joy in watching the lines take slow form: letter by letter accreting. It made me conscious of language as a physical entity, word by word and sentence by paragraph—the march of letters backward in the composing stick. kcits gnisopmoc eht ni drawkcab srettel fo hcram eht.

Mirror, mirror on the wall: who's the most facile of them all? To make a *pangram* into *pentagram,* we need only add that extraterrestrial E.T. To make a *manager* of *anagram* we change the "e" to "a." To make a *pangram* into *manager,* we change the "p" to "e." And so on and so forth. That clumsy child who mangled type was making words of *sword* or *sward* by changing an "o" to an "a."

Et set error.

"That was nice."

" 'Nice' comes from the Anglo-Saxon *nysse.* It means 'Not to know.' "

"A know-nothing?"

"Right. The opposite of *wysse.* A person in the know."

"That's nice."

"A *nice* distinction, yes. To make a nice distinction is to fuss or fidget with no consequential purpose."

"How many angels can you count, friend, on the head of a pin?"

"Twelve. Twelve thousand. Two."

"T'were to consider too curiously, to consider so."

"Now *you're* the one who's being nice."

"If you say so."

"A little more than kin."

"And less than kind."

It seems to me all writers—whether consciously, self-consciously, or unaware—deploy what they have learned from reading and adapt it to new use. (A not-so-subtle example thereof is my reference above to the language of *Hamlet,* where (1) Horatio reveals the limits of his speculative capacity: "T'were to consider too curiously . . ." and (2) the prince, in his first speech, describes the usurper, Claudius, as "A little more than kin . . .") There's a way in which each author is a student of what went before, and all of us absorb the work of predecessors. Whether the book on the shelf be the Bible or the plays of George Bernard Shaw or a Sears-Roebuck catalog, we slowly accrue alertness to what's on offer in print. In this regard there's "Nothing new under the sun," but that assertion must be wedded to Ezra Pound's injunction: "Make it new." The paradox inhering in those paired pronouncements is what powers each interpretation or revival of a work; in order to become a king the prince must also kill him, or so the story goes . . .

The line of descent and influence can be traced in novels nowadays: recent books that offer a new version of admired texts. Think of Michael Cunningham's *The Hours,* which pays homage to Virginia Woolf's *Mrs. Dalloway*. Or Zadie Smith's *On Beauty*, which finds its inspiration in E. M. Forster's *Howards End*. Or Jeffrey Eugenides's *The Marriage Plot*, derived from the action of Jane Austen's novels. To take just one more example, Patrick O'Brian's Aubrey and Maturin books constitute an uninterrupted foray into the imaginative discourse of a world at war two hundred years ago; large swatches of the story borrow from naval accounts.

In film, as well, the use of "backstory" is common. *Clueless* tells a contemporary version of Jane Austen's *Emma* that resonates once it is viewed as referencing that work. *Shakespeare in Love* is highly allusive, a good-humored salute to the language of Elizabethan England; its jokes require knowledge of the great plays and playwright it spoofs. *West Side Story* takes its scenario from *Romeo and Juliet*, several recent movies build on *West Side Story*, and so on down the line. The category "Original Screenplay" is no more Oscar-worthy than the category "Adaptation"—itself the title of a prize-winning film by Charlie Kaufman based on *The Orchid Thief* by Susan Orlean.

Broadway revivals are an annual affair, and most successful plays or musicals hire a second cast for the national tour. A "one-off" is a rarity, and what any playwright hopes for is an extended run. Yet even when the aim is full fidelity to an "original" production, the show will vary from night to night and actor to actor; no live performance replicates in every detail the previous or next. In this sense there's a single text—the written language preserved on the page—and a multitude of versions played out by a multitude of actors on the revival stage. Interpretative productions ("Let's do *Lysistrata* as a trans-gender manifesto!" "Let's do *Dr. Faustus* in antebellum costume!") are everywhere performed.

Imitation is, as well, a time-honored practice in verse. Robert Lowell used precisely that word to describe his own effort of translation from languages he read only a little and sometimes not at all. His book *Imitations* (1962) is a series of original poems inspired by and freely rendering the work of other poets. We call a sonnet "Petrarchan" or "Shakespearean" in honor of those who popularized the particular rhyme scheme and stanzaic pattern; we write in the "Miltonic" or "Spenserian" or "Eliotic" mode. The poet William Butler Yeats called apprenticeship a "singing school," and much of his own verse deploys traditional forms. Emily Dickinson and Walt Whitman—two widely admired "originals" of the nineteenth century—have influenced modern practitioners in direct lines of descent. Whether the genre be poetry or prose fiction, one task of the writing teacher is to point out antecedents: "Tom, you might want to look at what Dick did with this plot device; Harriet, you might (re)read the ballad by X, which your Y appears to follow." More often than not the student has no notion that it's been tried before.

"I want to copy you."
"Why?"
"I like your style."
"I like *your* style."
"They used to say, I think, 'Copy that.' "

"Copy *that!*"

"I *do* want to copy you."

"You too?"

"You two? You can say that again."

"This is ridiculous."

"No. But repetitive."

"You can say that again."

"I just did."

"Call me, Ishmael" is the opening sentence of a novel by Peter de Vries (1910–1993). In *The Vale of Laughter* (1967)—itself a comic reference to "the vale of tears"—he begins with, "Call me, Ishmael. Call me anytime, day or night." The narrator here refers, and not obliquely, to the first three words of Herman Melville's book about a peg-legged mariner and white whale. "Call me Ishmael"—one of the most famous opening lines in the history of literature—was a narrator's imperative to the nineteenth-century reader, sounding a clarion call. By inserting a comma into *Moby-Dick*'s first sentence, however, the twentieth-century author fashions a request from one character to another. No member of the crew of Melville's foredoomed whaling ship would have had a telephone. We get the joke.

De Vries used this strategy often. With several other titles—*Without a Stitch in Time* (1972), *I Hear America Swinging* (1976), and *Sauce for the Goose* (1981)—he took a phrase and twisted it for comic effect: adding or substituting a word or letter to a well-worn formula. Further, he titled a 1983 novel *Slouching towards*

Kalamazoo, which is a good-humored salute to William Butler Yeats's poem "The Second Coming," and its final question: "And what rough beast, its hour come round at last, / Slouches towards Bethlehem to be born?"

The beast is not so much born as wittily reborn, refashioned with a wink. Add a comma, change the name of a city, and two of the dark masterworks of English literature become an inside joke. When Joan Didion calls a collection of essays *Slouching towards Bethlehem,* her 1968 description of life in Southern California is titled without irony; we accept the reference at face value. Yeats and William Shakespeare—to take just two examples—have provided numberless titles for other authors' texts. I won't provide those authors' names or the dates of publication, because the list would grow too long, but here are just a few from Shakespeare: *Remembrance of Things Past, Salad Days, Nothing Like the Sun, Fools of Fortune, Pale Fire, Brave New World, Not so Deep as a Well, The Dogs of War, The Ides of March, The Sound and the Fury, The Moon Is Down, Cold Comfort Farm,* and *Infinite Jest.* Here are a few from Yeats: *Things Fall Apart, No Country for Old Men, The Golden Apples of the Sun, Coat upon a Stick, The Dying Animal, About My Table, When the Green Woods Laugh,* and *The Widening Gyre.*

Peter De Vries was marching to a different drum, and those readers who might recognize the phrase "a different drummer" may remember that it comes from *Walden* and Henry David Thoreau. There's a 1962 novel with *that* titular phrase by William Melvin Kelley, a 1971 RCA recording with the same phrase by Buddy Rich, the "Big Band" drummer; there's—to take, again, just two examples—a "Different Drummer Tattoo Parlor" in

Cape Girardeau, Missouri, and a cooking school, "Different Drummer's Kitchen," in Albany, New York. Our speech, our shops, our books and recordings all incorporate such referents: what we hear and say and write is almost unavoidably a form of repetition: "variation on a theme."

Try to write a paragraph with no such echo or association. Try to have a conversation using no word you've not used before. Try to listen to a song or look at a picture that reminds you of nothing you've previously heard or seen, and you'll perceive the problem. Everything is interlinked and has some prior resonance; all of us live with the past. We are creatures with retentive memories, and those who have no such facility—who live in the perpetual present—are limited and even, in a strict sense, maimed. Amnesia strips us of our memory, but the sentient individual is full of "echo or association," a phrase I've now used twice in this one paragraph. We repeat others and then repeat ourselves.

More broadly, we move from the copyist's task to our own original vision. All teaching strategies are predicated on instruction by way of repetition: *Repeat, class, after me.* No one seeks to be original when learning scales, or how to use a grindstone, or where the comma belongs in a dependent clause. We take for granted, as a culture, that certain skills need to be learned, and we do so via emulation, moving from the copycat's game of "Simon Says" to the youthful author's earnest effort: "Simon Writes." There's nothing shameful—indeed, much to be admired—in homage to a master or a rehearsal of what went before.

"SIMON SAYS: 'Raise your right arm!' "
We do.

"SIMON SAYS: 'Twirl your left hand!' "
We do.

"SIMON SAYS: 'Touch your nose.' "
We do.

"SIMON SAYS: 'Touch your ear.' "
We do.

"SIMON SAYS: 'Turn around.' "
We do.
"Turn around again."
We do, and therefore lose.

Let us consider the question in a more general way. What is this thing we celebrate called "originality," and why is the word "plagiarist" one of our actionable insults—particularly so in the academy? There was a risible fuss some time ago about First Lady Melania Trump's (or more accurately, her speechwriter's) arrogation of Michelle Obama's fine speech about the American Dream. But in all the fuss and bother there was no one who suggested the lady be sued for her no doubt inadvertent repetition, and Melania held no teaching job she would thereafter lose. Though plagiarism is a sin, it's also what we learn to do when first learning our shared language; we copy and repeat. All of us spend, I think—I myself certainly did—a good percentage of our youth as copycats or, more grandly, disciples: borrowing this one's accent, that one's way of wearing clothes, this one's dance step, and that one's opinions because we hope to make our model's moves our own. "When I grow up, I want to be like X or Y or Z." And at the end of this long process of admiration, emulation, imitation, there's a phrase for it: "Good writers borrow, great writers steal."

I'm at a loss, however, to know who first coined that bon mot. It has been severally attributed to Oscar Wilde in the nineteenth century (he gets the credit for every fine phrase not assigned to Mark Twain), or Picasso in the twentieth (though the brilliant Spaniard supposedly proclaimed "Good artists borrow, great artists steal" while doing so himself with some regularity from Goya and Velázquez). There's no evidence that either Wilde or Picasso made any such remark. More precisely, though still imprecisely, T. S. Eliot did in fact assert (in *The Sacred Wood: Essays on Poetry and Criticism*, 1920), "Immature poets borrow, mature poets steal."

Some years ago, I published a teaching text called *The Sincerest Form: Writing Fiction by Imitation* (2003). The title derives from the widely quoted line "Imitation is the sincerest form of flattery." Few of us remember, though, that the phrase was composed by a fellow called George Caleb Colton (1780–1832), who wrote—in a book of aphorisms called *The Lacon*—"Imitation is the sincerest of flattery." He himself makes no mention of form. It's implicit in the idea, yes, but we render it explicit. So whether we've inaccurately quoted Colton or Eliot—who deployed the terms "immature" and "mature," not "good" and "great," when writing about poets—we make into our common parlance, and coin of the verbal realm, what some forgotten or celebrated someone coined way back when.

In time to come, I'd venture, a hundred folk will use the phrase "catch-22" for every one who knows that it was once the title of a book by Joseph Heller. Most of us know such phrases as "nature and nurture" or "Yankee Doodle Dandy," but few remember their first use in what would become familiar speech. Francis Galton and George M. Cohan, for those who insist on attribution, are credited with the respective three-word formulae, but the founder of eugenics and the Broadway showman are no longer with us. Their language, however, lives on.

Metaphoric speech is difficult to track. Who first described the snake as the embodiment of evil or decided that a dove or lamb should serve as a symbol of peace? Was it Homer or some unnamed predecessor who imagined "rosy-fingered dawn" and "the wine-dark sea"? And wit is just as hard to source: who first invented "knock-knock" jokes or the story that begins, "A man walks into a bar"? Long before the world of Twitter feed or Instagram (both newly current terms), a joke would spread like wildfire from friend to friend and town to country, told happily and often and almost always without ascription. A few routines—"Who's on first?" or "Take my wife"—are attached to the comedians who made them popular, but Abbott and Costello or Henny Youngman used writers who have vanished from the scene. You cannot copyright titles, but how would or should one go about a claim of ownership for phrases such as "yellow-bellied" or "hunky-dory" or, less colloquially, "high-minded" and "good as gold"?

There's a test, still, in certain schools, where the student is asked to identify—on the basis of a paragraph or two, a stanza or three—the name of the progenitor of an unattributed text. It's the dream of writers to be thus recognizable, to be idiosyncratic and identifiable in a way that argues authorship, even if the piece be left unsigned. No one else could compose this, we declare, in that particular way. And expertise consists of saying. "Ah yes, this fragment must come from the pen of George Eliot, that canvas is surely a Peter Paul Rubens" or—contrarily—"No, that couldn't be Laurence Sterne, that wouldn't be Salvador Dalí; the artistic signature's not right." Think of those musicians who sue each other over authorship of a brief musical phrase, a set of chord changes, or—astonishingly, of late—the painter who had to defend himself in a lawsuit brought by a collector, who had been sold a forgery of the selfsame painter's work. He said, "I never painted that," and the outraged collector-investor said, in effect, "Yes, you did." It's a vexed topic, always; trouble awaits the dancer who executes a different step from those around her in the chorus line, or the violist who plays *forte* while the rest of the string section is playing *piano* as per the conductor's baton. Although we exalt originality, we call it into question every day.

With the passage of time, moreover, copyright laws and the ownership of language come to matter less. Nomenclature—branding—loses its importance. Attribution fades. To quote two otherwise dissimilar writers, we move from Shakespeare's "A rose by any other name would smell as sweet" to Gertrude Stein's "A rose is a rose is a rose." Both these statements argue that the thing itself is irreducible, and the name by which we know it is, if not irrelevant, a secondary concern. What do we really know of Sophocles or Sappho or Marie de France or even J. D. Salinger and the reclusive Thomas Pynchon; what if anything do we know of the authors of the Beowulf epic or the Bible and Mahābhārata and *The Pillow Book of Sei Shōnagon*?

More important, perhaps, who cares? Why should it matter that Ernest Hemingway wore a beard and Emily Dickinson a white dress; what difference does it make to our understanding of their excellence to know that the aforementioned T. S. Eliot was a not-so-closeted anti-Semite and Franz Kafka a practicing Jew? It can be useful to know the private lives of public men and women, for there are ways in which the former does inform the latter. But in some central way the dream of common parlance is a dream of anonymity, and to enter into our collective discourse— think "catch-22," think "Yankee Doodle Dandy," think "nature and nurture"—is not to need to be named.

In his great short story "Pierre Menard, Author of the Quixote," Jorge Luis Borges suggests that his character Pierre Menard, far from being derivative, is in fact superior to Miguel de Cervantes because, knowing what that author knew, he can nonetheless repeat it. Yet he does so with an enlarged consciousness, with everything echoic and, in effect, doubly resonant. This incorporation of the past is essential, I think, to both the present and future of verbal art. It's impossible, or at the least implausible, to be original from first to final line. In human if not genomic terms, there's nothing new under the sun. I could, I suppose, write a novel that deals with the love affair and mixed resulting DNA of two monkeys with a banana peel as a fetishistic worship-object in a space capsule while the Astronaut and Astronaughty catapult through the universe, traversing Mars and Venus—but who would want to read that, and what's the point of doing something no one else bothered to do? There's a difference, in effect, between originality and the merely new.

"Can we change, now, the terms of engagement?"
"Why not?"
"Let's call it a marriage instead."
"Of?"
"Forme et fond. Style and substance."
"Matter and manner?"
"Correct."
"That was nice."
"You're repeating yourself."
" 'Make it new.' "

I've been describing all this in general terms; it is instead a series of specifics that must be tracked case by case. When the writer attains her or his own voice—or so it almost always seems—it comes through rigorous exercise and a set of practiced scales. It's a matter of manner, less substance than style, what the French call *forme* not *fond*. Consider the difference between these two opposing rhetorics, though in essence they say the same thing: "I ain't sure you my main squeeze no mo'," and "Cyril's in dubiety with reference to his earlier infatuation."

Or, "Stand and deliver, stranger, that I might know your ancestry and rank," and "Yo, bro,' wozzup?"

Montrose Reg. Library Dist.
320 S. 2nd St.
Montrose, CO 81401

These examples are extreme, of course, but within that range is a world of tonality and intonation, a set of signature styles. "Howdy" and "Hey there" and "Top of the mornin' " all deliver the same message. So do "Good morrow, mistress," and "Get your sorry ass up," and "Rise and shine." Therefore which diction we elect is like a set of fingerprints or snowflakes: individuated, irreducible, ours and ours alone. Yet diction too may change. Raymond Queneau, in his *Exercises in Style* (translated from the French to English in 1958) describes the same encounter between two people on a bus one hundred times, and in one hundred separate ways; the styles are wholly various but the substance stays the same.

Think of the difference between "orotund" and "rotund" or "parable" and "arable," or, even more lengthily, "platitudinarian" and "latitudinarian." Or, come to that, "further" and "farther" and "father" and "lather" and "later" and "eater"—all single-letter shifts that entail a shift of meaning. (When thick-fingered, and setting language manually for that high-school printing press, I garbled such meanings continually in an inadvertent game of word-golf and hapless arrangement of prose. Pose. Rose.) It's the composer's key change, the painter's altered perspective, a problem the type-setter tries not to have when shifting a word from the spoken to set. To "fabricate" is both to make and lie. We work our way down the printed page and work our way up through the ranks.

This last word, too, is double-edged; when King Claudius declares, "Oh my offense is rank" (act 3, scene 3), he means both that he's violated the proper hierarchy of things in ascending to the kingship by killing Hamlet's father, and that the deed stinks.

There are two meanings equally to the word "offense"; one is approbative (as in "he went on the offense") and one the reverse (as in "she took offense"). Usage varies; context varies; to have a strong offense in football or war is not to be offensive, but it's appropriate to fend off what offends.

Some of us are autodidacts; others earn degrees. Some of us have private tutors; others go to class. (Note how the notion of a private tutorial entails the suggestion of "class"; it has the ring of anachrony, privilege, and, to a degree, of degree.) The very idea of an MFA "degree" in creative writing is recent and, in the history of art, irrelevant—though some might *dis*agree. And *diss* with an additional "s" means something else again. I'm trying to suggest, of course, that our language shifts and shifts; it's constantly reborn. A native speaker of English today would have no better chance of understanding the native speaker of English in the year 1100 than he or she would have of understanding a speaker in Oslo or Seoul. The *Oxford English Dictionary*—that arbiter of standards and repository of collective discourse—is always adding words or relegating them instead to the status: *obs.* Obsolete. Delete.

❧

"Hello."

"Hell*o*."

"Good morning."

"Afternoon. It's five o'clock."

"Good evening."

"Make up your mind, please, can't you? It can't be all at once."

"Why not?"

"Time is sequential, not simultaneous. It's morning, noon, then night."

"Why not?"

"You're being, like that children's game, repetitive."

"You're being, like that children's game, repetitive."

"This can't go on."

"It can."

The evolution of spoken speech has been long established, and verbal gamesmanship was with us from the start. As Shakespeare amply demonstrates, our language has its roots in sonority, the heard and repeated arrangement of words. English was conveyed by *oral* utterance and retained in *aural* memory long before the invention and widespread use of print. The way to remember the lines of a play was to hear not read them, and repetition and rote learning were for many centuries the way to acquire a text.

This, however, entailed some confusion when it came time to write the speeches down. The first printed version of Shakespeare's plays (The Folio Edition of 1623) came seven years after his death, and its author was not present to supervise the process. Let's stay with the great tragedy I referenced earlier. When Hamlet cries "Oh that this too too sullied flesh would melt . . ." (act 1, scene 2), did he in fact say "solid flesh"? The received version is "sullied," but there's an alternate reading of "solid,"—or even perhaps, as in Queen Cleopatra's "salad days," the metaphoric "salad flesh." My own preferred usage is "solid," because it seems like a good punning reference to the extra pounds put on in later years by the actor Richard Burbage, Shakespeare's leading man. He had, it would seem, grown portly, and the playwright urged him (when preparing the role of the stripling prince) to lose weight.

Further, there's a tale about sexual rivalry between those two prominent members of the same theatrical troupe. That group, first known as the Lord Chamberlain's Men under Queen Elizabeth, became the King's Men after the succession of James I. At some point during a performance of *Richard III,* Shakespeare and the actor Richard Burbage both courted an available lady and were vying for her favor. They were after much more than her hand.

According to the story—from lawyer John Manningham's diary, in 1602—when Burbage knocked on the fair damsel's door he found a note: "William the Conqueror was before Richard III!" It's a fine joke, a comic reference to English history as well as one of Shakespeare's history plays, but almost surely untrue. (Would one suitor leave a written boast for another to discover outside a lady's boudoir; would the joke about "William the Conqueror" have had contemporary currency; was the playwright, when in London, interested in the company of ladies—or rather in those who portrayed them at the Globe, young men?) Who first coined the sly anecdote that Manningham wrote down?

"I've said this before."
"I've *read* this before."
"I wrote this before."

"Where? When?"

"Repetition is the essence of wit."

"Is that a quote?"

"What?"

" 'Repetition is the essence of wit.' "

"Q.E.D."

"Call me, Ishmael," is the opening sentence of a novel by Peter de Vries (1910–1993). In *The Vale of Laughter* (1967)—itself a comic reference to "the vale of tears"—he begins with, "Call me, Ishmael. Call me anytime, day or night." The narrator here refers, and not obliquely, to the first three words of Herman Melville's book about a peg-legged mariner and white whale. "Call me Ishmael"—one of the most famous opening lines in the history of literature—was a narrator's imperative to the nineteenth-century reader, sounding a clarion call. By inserting a comma into *Moby-Dick*'s first sentence, however, the twentieth-century author fashions a request from one character to another. No member of the crew of Melville's foredoomed whaling ship would have had a telephone. We get the joke.

De Vries used this strategy often. With several other titles—*Without a Stitch in Time* (1972), *I Hear America Swinging* (1976), and *Sauce for the Goose* (1981)—he took a phrase and twisted it for comic effect: adding or substituting a word or letter to a well-worn formula. Further, he titled a 1983 novel, *Slouching towards Kalamazoo,* which is a good-humored salute to William Butler Yeats's poem, "The Second Coming," and its final question: "And what rough beast, its hour come round at last, / Slouches towards Bethlehem to be born?"

The beast is not so much born as wittily reborn, refashioned with a wink. Add a comma, change the name of a city, and two of the dark masterworks of English literature become an inside joke. Yeats and William Shakespeare—to take just two examples—have provided numberless titles for other authors' texts. I won't provide those authors' names or the dates of publication, because the list would grow too long, but here are just a few from Shakespeare: *Brave New World, Cold Comfort Farm, The Dogs of War, Fools of Fortune, The Ides of March, Infinite Jest, The Moon Is Down, Nothing Like the Sun, Not so Deep as a Well, Pale Fire, Remembrance of Things Past, Salad Days, The Sound and the Fury.* Here are a few from Yeats: *Coat upon a Stick, The Dying Animal, The Golden Apples of the Sun, No Country for Old Men, Things Fall Apart, When the Green Woods Laugh,* and *The Widening Gyre.*

Peter De Vries was marching to a different drum, and those readers who might recognize the phrase "a different drummer" may remember that it comes from *Walden* and Henry David Thoreau. There's a 1962 novel with *that* titular phrase by William Melvin Kelley, a 1971 RCA recording with that same phrase by Buddy Rich, the "Big Band" drummer; there's—to take, again, just two examples—a "Different Drummer Tattoo Parlor" in Cape Girardeau, Missouri, and a cooking school, "Different Drummer's Kitchen," in Albany, New York. Our speech, our shops, our books and recordings each incorporate such referents. What we hear and say and write is almost unavoidably a form of repetition: "variation on a theme."

How long did it take you, dear reader, to know that you've read this before? Did you recognize it from the opening phrase, the opening line, first sentence, paragraph or page? Did you turn back to the previous instance and then contrast and compare? Did you think it an error of printing or copy-editing or simply a willed gesture on the author's part? Did you agree the repetition's clever or find it, instead, a bore? Did you note where the language has changed?

We call such change *revision,* and each revision a draft. I cut, for example, the sentence: "When Joan Didion calls a collection of essays *Slouching towards Bethlehem,* her 1968 description of life in Southern California is titled without irony; we accept the reference at face value." On second thought, I changed the order of the borrowed titles from Shakespeare and Yeats by alphabetizing them and, on third thought, dropped the title, *About My Table,* from the listings of the latter—since, as it happens, that title is one I myself used for a collection of short stories in 1983 (*vide* Chapter 1). I changed the word "all" to "each" in the previously final sentence prior to the colon: "each incorporate such referents." And, in order to avoid a doubling usage of that punctuation mark, the colon (of which, in a single sentence, there are rarely two), I used a period instead. So what had been the "final sentence" is now the penultimate one . . .

This sort of tinkering and syntax scratching is familiar to any author who presses on her or his language as though it were a bruise. ("This sort of tinkering is familiar to every author; we try to simplify." "That sort of tinkering?" "This sort of fiddling?" "That sort of syntax scratching?" "This process is familiar to every author; we try to simplify.") But vision and revision hardly seem to belong to the same category of labor; what one writes the first time through bears only a distant resemblance to what one writes the last. I composed the original version some six or seven times in the attempt to get it right; I waited a week and rewrote it, as per the above. I'll no doubt do so once or thrice again before the thing sees print, and there will be other eyes—friends, editors, copy-editors—to scrutinize the text. It might not survive the final draft; it might, as does the sentence about Joan Didion, lie on the cutting-room floor. Virginia Woolf instructed us to "kill your little darlings," but she herself was childless and often wrote at speed.

I had typed out, to start with, " 'Call me, Ishmael,' is the first sentence of *The Vale of Laughter* (1967), a novel by Peter de Vries (1910–1993.)" Then I got rid of the parenthetical dates and in the next draft restored them. Then I broke the opening sentence in half and added a reference to the vale of tears and made of that first sentence two. I decided not to mention that I'd known the author's son, that my great friend and colleague, Charles Baxter, also admires Peter de Vries, or that the dead writer seems to me unjustly forgotten and ready for revival. I asked myself how many of my readers would make the instant connection to *Moby-Dick* or if I needed to point it up, point it out.

The point is the comma, of course. But I'd used the word "point" three times in eight words—now four in twenty—and didn't want to belabor it; a joke that requires explaining is a joke ill-conceived, ill-delivered. I tried out a discourse on humor, on the even-more-forgotten S. J. Perelman, also an important figure from the period. I wondered how much of De Vries's biography and bibliography to include.

For days I cut and shaped the paragraphs, engaging in what scholars call *variora,* variations on a theme. In the end I settled for the lines above (and, of course, its repetition), because the point is not its excellence or lack thereof, but the fact that the original and its imitation are two peas in a ppod.

Copy that.

3 five texts

The enterprise of writing is, often, associated in titular fashion with a system of belief: consider such texts as *The Book of Kells* or *The Book of Mormon* or *The Tibetan Book of the Dead.* Think of that colloquial description of the Old and the New Testament as, in effect, "The Good Book." "In the beginning was the Word," we read, and language wrests shape from chaos: expressions of devotion are by their adepts spelled out.

But I want here to focus on secular titles—ones that influence our daily behavior and thought. In the familiar and somewhat arbitrary opposition between "sacred" and "profane," I plan to look at work from the workaday world. There are a multitude of texts, and my list is almost implausibly truncate; it could extend at length. One could argue, for example, that the tale of Marco Polo's travels or Hakluyt's Voyages fueled the desire, in the West, for exploration; one could claim *The Tale of Genji*—arguably the first novel in the history of literature, composed by Lady Murasaki in the early eleventh century—made a difference in the way we understand Japan. One could pick *L'Immoraliste* or *The Second Sex* or the writings of Sigmund Freud; one could choose *Don Quixote* or *The Prince* or *The Wealth of Nations* or *Faust*.

Such books are legion, and the list reveals its maker. Another reader might assert, as did the poet Ezra Pound, that "Literature is news that stays news." Poetry gave and gives us, say, the articulated vision of Ovid or Byron or Sappho or Sylvia Plath. As the first major genre of artistic discourse (after that came drama, and after that, prose) the form predates writing itself; generation after generation learned, via oral transmission, the history of those who went before. Lord Byron's friend and fellow practitioner Percy Bysshe Shelley famously called poets "the unacknowledged legislators of the world," and there are those who claim that poetry is the crucial witness to society. It's what endures when other written records fade away. Walt Whitman and Emily Dickinson tell us much about the landscape of nineteenth-century America, though the first was a committed wanderer and the second a reclusive stay-at-home.

This holds true for the more recent genre, prose fiction, as well. We know about pre-revolutionary Russia, for example, because of *War and Peace* or *Anna Karenina;* what we know of Charles Dickens's London we understand in part because of his descriptions. *The Adventures of Huckleberry Finn* evokes pre–Civil War Missouri and the deep South; *Remembrance of Things Past* portrays a segment of society in early twentieth-century France. In the brief discussions that follow—admittedly idiosyncratic in terms of their selection—I want to try to demonstrate why writing mattered to the culture and should matter to us still. The five examples are ranked in order of chronology, not comparative importance:

The Communist Manifesto, Karl Marx and Friedrich Engels, 1848

Uncle Tom's Cabin, Harriet Beecher Stowe, 1852

The Origin of the Species, Charles Darwin, 1859

"J'Accuse," Émile Zola, 1898

Lady Chatterley's Lover, D. H. Lawrence, 1928

The reader will have noticed that the period spanned is just eighty years, a blink of the eye in an extended overview of written composition. Each of the texts is Western, although from four separate countries—Great Britain, twice, America and France and Germany once each. Five of these six authors are male; all of them are white. Two of the titles require translation, and the point of this discussion is not artistic excellence but the efficacy of the prose; their manner of expression counts less than what's conveyed. Elsewhere in *Why Writing Matters,* my close focus is on language; here the topic is substance, not style.

Two of these are novels, one a scientific inquiry. Two are short works: the first a pamphlet of sociological theory that helped engender revolution, the next an "open letter" published by an out-raged activist. The five texts have in common a desire to call attention to and alter old assumptions and entrenched institutions—whether those of slavery or anti-Semitism, class structure and economic in-equality, or sexual behavior and the evolution of our species. All five had a profound effect on their intended audience; each did intend an audience and were written with self-conscious awareness of reaction and result. In the aftermath of publication, society would change.

I could, with almost equal justification, have listed Thomas Paine's *Common Sense* (1776) or Erica Jong's *Fear of Flying* (1973) as alternatives to the fourth and fifth of these titles, but the point of such a catalog is not to be comprehensive so much as represen-tative. And a disclaimer should be offered as to the discussions that follow; I cannot hope and do not pretend to deal with the five texts in depth. Yet these examples seem to me to demonstrate that writing matters, and in five separate ways.

Workers of the world, unite.

Religion is the opiate of the people.

The proletarians have nothing to lose but their chains!

These are three of the most famous sentences in the history of writing. Some would call them "infamous," and the lines have been translated; the original German pronouncements are less widely known. The first of these, in fact, is the decidedly less catchy "Proletarier aller Länder vereinigt Euch!" and much has been gained in translation. The second statement, from a *Contribution to the Critique of Hegel's Philosophy of Right* (a work published in full only after his death) was composed by Marx in 1844. The third is often paraphrased or translated as direct address to the reader as listener: "You have nothing to lose but your chains!"

The first and last of these come from the brief work known as *The Communist Manifesto,* co-authored by Karl Marx and Friedrich Engels in 1848. That document has had, over time, an almost-improbable outreach and political afterlife. Most notably in Tsarist Russia and what it would evolve into—Soviet Russia and the Union of Soviet Socialist Republics—the twenty-three-page pamphlet (in what became unnumbered editions and more than eighty languages) has defined the ideology of millions.

The work was commissioned by a congress of the "Communist League" meeting in London in 1847; Marx and Engels, recent members of that league, wrote separate first drafts. The draft composed by Engels came in the form of a catechism, with twenty-five questions and answers; Marx was, it seems, the principal author of the final version, whose full original title is "Manifesto of the Communist Party." Yet it's important here to note that the pamphlet has paired names on the title page; unlike the four following instances, it's a collaborative work. Engels, with characteristic modesty, gave most of the credit to Marx, who drafted the finished text in six weeks, but this is not an instance of a singular vision or voice; the language and the ideation—appropriately enough, given the message—were shared.

The *Manifesto* appeared relatively early in the authors' respective careers. Marx died in 1883, Engels in 1895, and each produced much else. The "profound effect" referred to earlier took a long time to come to fruition. But their analysis of the inevitable conflict between members of the bourgeoisie and proletariat had an enduring influence on national and international systems, and it's worth pondering "why writing matters" in such a case.

The document was not, of course, produced *in vacuo*. Mid-century Europe was everywhere convulsive; the year 1848 was one of revolutions, or attempted revolutions, in Sicily, France, and what would become the nation-states of Italy and Germany as well as Scandinavia and the Austro-Hungarian Empire. These were not coordinated movements so much as local uprisings, and their political results were less consequential than their enduring social impact; the barricades may have been stormed and the leaders imprisoned or killed, but the sense of outrage at inequity and economic inequality endured. This was a slow-building as well as combustible admixture of provocation and grievance; the French Revolution had not happened in a day, nor would the several monarchies be disbanded overnight. Still, it's fair to say that 1848 was a watershed year, and Europe would not look or be the same thereafter.

Lasting reforms included the start of representative democracy in the Netherlands, the end of absolute monarchy in Denmark, and the eradication of serfdom in Hungary and Austria. The nation-states of Germany and Italy, too, began to take their contemporary shape and form. It's difficult to yoke all this to the image of the plump, full-bearded Karl Marx who found himself exiled to England and would spend long years in the British Museum's library, composing *Das Kapital* (1867). Was he the cause or the result of a collective shift of consciousness; was he the inventor, or simply a principal purveyor, of the system of thought we now call, eponymously, Marxism?

These are questions easier to ask than answer, and my field is neither sociology nor politics. But it seems safe to say that *The Communist Manifesto* heralded a major change in Western and then world behavior—a credo and secular bible for those who'd been "enchained." After its publication and slow dissemination, the "proletarians of the world" had their own shared version of a sacred text.

Friedrich Hegel, in *The Phenomenology of Mind* (1807), had proposed the process of a dialectic—of each idea engendering its own opposition, of thesis and antithesis resulting in a newly established synthesis. Hegel had borrowed Immanuel Kant's notion of "antinomies" and used it to describe the progress of history, but his was a largely abstract argument, since he believed that what impelled the dialectic were ideas. Marx and Engels deployed the concept of the dialectic so that it was driven not by ideas but by "historical materialism." By this they meant that it was the change in the technical means of production rather than that of ideas which drove the process of class formation and struggle. This last is omnipresent throughout history, and would therefore continue.

In the relatively recent past, aristocrat and serf had been bound together, interdependent, and from that opposition arose the bourgeoisie. From the rise and predominance of the bourgeoisie, in turn, emerged the proletariat, and this historical dialectic would culminate in a new synthesis: communism. The manifesto begins with the line: "A specter is haunting Europe—the specter of Communism." That specter haunts Europe still.

Much of the prose is turgid. The sentences that follow are examples of Marx and Engels at their most sententious and least compelling. I pick them at near random; there are many more:

> The various interests and conditions of life within the ranks of the proletariat are more and more equalized, in proportion as machinery obliterates all distinctions of labour, and nearly everywhere reduces wages to the same low level.

> The Communists, therefore, are on the one hand, practically, the most advanced and resolute section of the working-class parties of every country, that section which pushes forward all others; on the other hand, theoretically, they have over the great mass of the proletariat the advantage of clearly understanding the line of march, the conditions, and the ultimate general results of the proletarian movement.

> The robe of speculative cobwebs, embroidered with flowers of rhetoric, steeped in the dew of sickly sentiment, this transcendental robe in which the German Socialists wrapped their sorry "eternal truths," all skin and bone, served to wonderfully increase the sale of their goods amongst such a public.

And so on. The manifesto itself was an irrelevance to the upheavals and uprisings of 1848, and only when espoused by Vladimir Lenin and the Russian Revolution of 1917 did it gain widespread readership—an audience enlarged on years later by Chairman Mao Zedong. Without such sponsorship, it would no doubt have languished unopened on the shelves of libraries or in second-hand bookstores unread. By contrast, the national anthem of France, *La Marseillaise* (with its call to arms, "Aux armes, citoyens"), and the opening phrase of the Declaration of Independence ("When in the course of human events") had been applauded and repeated from the start. Yet the three texts have in common an enduring life in language, and those who framed the sentences—even, as with *La Marseillaise,* the more or less anonymous author Claude Joseph Rouget de Lisle—live on.

Political campaigns and advertising slogans and television programs all desire to coin or mint (note how these verbs refer to "currency") an unforgettable phrase. Elections have been won or lost because of formulae; "Tippecanoe and Tyler too!" or "I like Ike" are only two examples of such rhymed sloganeering. We can't of course know what would have happened if "Ike's" campaign had instead proclaimed: "Dwight David Eisenhower for President!" but odds are his victory margin would have been smaller. Most readers of the *New York Times* applaud its long-established motto: "All the news that's fit to print." And everywhere our discourse is studded with catch-phrases: *Where's the beef?* and *Just do it, Lock her up,* and *Build the wall!* to quote a very few.

Marx and Engels were not the first to use the short-form declaration of a manifesto. But they did popularize it, and in the next century such avant-garde publications as those by Filippo Tommaso Marinetti (*The Futurist Manifesto,* 1909), Vladimir Mayakovsky (*A Slap in the Face of Public Taste,* 1913), and André Breton (*Manifesto of Surrealism,* 1924), were patterned on the model the German authors deployed. So the three sentences with which this section starts (no matter in which language or how roughly translated) have burned their way into collective consciousness. They have done so all the more ineradicably because once written down.

On the face of it, a book such as *Uncle Tom's Cabin* (1852) would not seem a likely agent of change; few texts, however, have had greater impact on the country in which they appeared. Whatever the aesthetic value of Harriet Beecher Stowe's novel, the political and sociological impact proved immense. It's hard to calculate with arithmetical precision the effect of a work of fiction, but the Civil War was at least to some degree occasioned by her graphic account of slavery, and its institutionalized horrors. Though this may be apocryphal, President Lincoln was said a decade later to have greeted Ms. Stowe at the White House by saying, "Is this the little woman who made this great war?"

Harriet Beecher Stowe (1811–1896) was born in Litchfield, Connecticut, and died in nearby Hartford; her family was prominent, and she seemed content at first to hide her light under the bushel of her famous father and brother—the Calvinist preacher Lyman Beecher and, foremost among her dozen siblings, the abolitionist Henry Ward Beecher. Having made her home in Cincinnati, she married a widowed teacher, Calvin Stowe, who soon accepted a faculty position at Bowdoin College in Brunswick, Maine. There she established contact with Gamaliel Bailey, the editor of an anti-slavery newspaper, writing to him (on March 9, 1851) that "the time is come when even a woman or a child who can speak a word for freedom and humanity is bound to speak."

In Cincinnati the writer had encountered fugitive slaves who had escaped from or through Kentucky; the death of a young son may also have instructed her in what it means to lose a child, and as the wife, daughter, and sister of Protestant clergymen, her religious sensibility powered her account of suffering and sacrifice. As she told Bailey with impassioned prescience when proposing her serial magazine pieces, "The time is come."

At the age of forty-one, Harriet Beecher Stowe began publication in *The National Era* with a story called "The Man That Was a Thing." Soon enough the subtitle changed to "Life among the Lowly," and the set of articles was published in book form on March 20, 1852. In short order, *Uncle Tom's Cabin* sold an almost-unprecedented 300,000 copies in America, and more than a million in Great Britain. As David S. Reynolds reports in his *Mightier Than the Sword,* this came at a period when books were routinely shared or read aloud—so those who encountered Stowe's work may have numbered ten times the amount of copies sold; after the Bible, *Uncle Tom* was the second-best-selling book of the nineteenth century.

Whatever its artistic merits—Leo Tolstoy praised it, James Baldwin disdained it—the novel brought to light a deep-rooted and, it would prove, irreconcilable disagreement between the North and South. (In smaller ways but much the same fashion, such books as Upton Sinclair's *The Jungle* and Rachel Carson's *Silent Spring* would later be part of what we now call "the national conversation.") This fiction-cum-tract and moral sermon proved a central document in the *agon* over the Fugitive Slave Act of 1850; its vivid representation of the misery of slavery and the tyranny of ownership was everywhere discussed.

As the opening paragraph of her Preface asserts:

The scenes of this story, as its title indicates, lie among a race hitherto ignored by the associations of polite and refined society: an exotic race, whose ancestors, born beneath a tropic sun, brought with them, and perpetuated for their descendants, a character so essentially unlike the hard and dominant Anglo-Sax race, as for many years to have won from it only misunderstanding and contempt.

Harriet Beecher Stowe's imagination was, in effect, allegorical. The figure of the beautiful Eliza, who escapes from bounty hunters with her baby in her arms, is a more or less direct evocation of the Madonna and Child. Uncle Tom himself—with his almost superhuman willingness to forgive his enemies—is a Christ figure, and Simon Legree (soon to become an eponymous incarnation of evil) is, if not the Devil, a fiend. There's the mysterious and brooding Cassy, who belongs to Legree; there's the figure—based on Daniel Webster—of Senator Bird of Ohio, who represents the possibility of redemptive change. His heart is melted by Eliza, who begs for asylum while she is "cut and bleeding" as a runaway in his kitchen, and he springs into action to save her from the bounty hunters who would take advantage of and profit from "the real presence of distress."

Here are a few further quotations from the text. It's a long book, full of characters, preachment, and action, and I won't attempt to contextualize these lines. But they give some sense of rhetoric and the morality expressed:

Scenes of blood and cruelty are shocking to our ear and heart. What man has nerve to do, man has not nerve to hear.

"But now what? Why, now comes my master, takes me right away from my work, and my friends, and all I like, and grinds me down into the very dirt! And why? Because, he says, I forgot who I was; he says, to teach me that I am only a nigger! After all, and last of all, he comes between me and my wife, and says I shall give her up, and live with another woman. And all this your laws give him power to do, in spite of God or man. Mr. Wilson, look at it! There isn't one of all these things, that have broken the hearts of my mother and my sister, and my wife and myself, but your laws allow, and give every man power to do, in Kentucky, and none can say to him nay! Do you call these the laws of my country? Sir, I haven't any country, anymore than I have any father. But I'm going to have one. I don't want anything of your country, except to be let alone,—to go peaceably out of it; and when I get to Canada, where the laws will own me and protect me, that shall be my country, and its laws I will obey. But if any man tries to stop me, let him take care, for I am desperate. I'll fight for my liberty to the last breath I breathe. You say your fathers did it; if it was right for them, it is right for me!"

"I am braver than I was because I have lost all; and he who has nothing to lose can afford all risks."

But it is often those who have least of all in this life whom He chooseth for the kingdom. Put thy trust in Him and no matter what befalls thee here, He will make all right hereafter.

By the end of her life, Harriet Beecher Stowe would publish some thirty books of fiction, travel memoirs, articles, and letters. Among her other novels are such titles as *The Minister's Wooing* and *Oldtown Folks,* but none of them approached the reach of *Uncle Tom.* Her gift, as she told Bailey, was pictorial; she claimed that "my vocation is simply that of *painter,*" and the image of Uncle Tom (in jigsaw puzzles, cartoons, dolls, stage shows, burlesques, and film) remains with us. The name itself has come to stand for something very different than that of a character in a novel, but it is part of common parlance now and will not go away.

~~~

Charles Darwin (1809–1882) did not see himself primarily as a writer, at least not at the start. He was the fifth of six children born to a wealthy society doctor and a daughter of Josiah Wedgewood, the purveyor of English bone china. Raised in privilege, he too planned to be a doctor. The medical curriculum at the University of Edinburgh, however, failed to compel his attention, and at his father's urging he matriculated in Cambridge instead, becoming increasingly attracted to the study of botany and beetles. After graduating with a bachelor of arts degree and the vague intention of a career as an Anglican county parson, he took a brief trip with one of his teachers to study geological strata in Wales. Next—again at the suggestion of a teacher—he joined up as gentleman-naturalist on the voyage of HMS *Beagle,* under the command of Captain Robert Fitzroy. They set sail on December 27, 1831, on a trip that was projected to take two years; they would stay abroad for five.

That trip has been exhaustively documented, first by Charles Darwin himself. His *The Voyage of the Beagle* (formally published as *Journal and Remarks* in 1839) brought him national attention and, to a degree, broke his health. The nature of his illness has been much debated (a tropical infection, exhaustion brought on by overwork, neurasthenia, Ménières disease, Chagas disease, lactose intolerance?), but it had the effect of keeping him at home for much of his life thereafter. And, for much of his life, at his desk.

So the young gentleman with a penchant for riding and shooting, then the adolescent botanizer, then the world-traveler, became a married quasi-recluse with a private library, an extensive correspondence—more than fifteen thousand letters have survived—and a scientific thesis that it would take years to develop, then express. That thesis would upend the system of entrenched belief about the origins of man and nature of mankind; it brought a major paradigm shift to our collective understanding of what it means to be human. His theory of evolution is too well known to discuss extensively here; ever since the publication of *On the Origin of Species* (with the elaborate subtitle *By Means of Natural Selection, or The Preservation of Favoured Races in the Struggle for Life*), it has been a bedrock of scientific thought. In retrospect it seems as though his reasoning was pre-ordained, a steady forward march to a foregone conclusion. What I want to stress, instead, are the writer's uncertainties: his wavering and havering as to publication (on November 24, 1859), his doubts about the project and its effects on religious orthodoxy, his agonized revisions—he kept a "vomitorium" near his writing chair—and his ensuing rush to print.

A colleague, Alfred Wallace, had much the same intuition as to what we've come to call "natural selection." At times his work was almost as collaborative with Darwin as that of Marx and Engels; at times the two men were competitive and jockeying for first place in the race to document the "tangled bank" or "tree of life." Darwin was, as noted, a gentleman of private means; Wallace had to earn his keep as a collector and then merchant of rare specimens; much of what he harvested—when sent back to England and subject to shipwreck—was lost.

It's a complicated story, and not wholly germane to the topic at hand, but the second paragraph of Darwin's Introduction to his published magnum opus tells at least part of the tale:

> My work is now (1859) nearly finished. But it will take me many more years to complete it, and as my health is far from strong, I have been urged to publish this Abstract. I have more especially been induced to do this, as Mr. Wallace, who is now studying the natural history of the Malay archipelago, has arrived at almost exactly the same general conclusions that I have on the origin of species. In 1858 he sent me a memoir on this subject, with a request that I would forward it to Sir Charles Lyell, who sent it to the Linnean Society, and it is published in the third volume of the Journal of that society. Sir C. Lyell and Dr. Hooker, who both knew of my work—the latter having read my sketch of 1844—honored me by thinking it advisable to publish, with Mr. Wallace's excellent memoir, some brief extracts from my manuscripts.

As his grandson, Charles G. Darwin, would observe in the Preface to an edition of the work more than a hundred years later (1963), "In the opinion of many experts the general thinking of man about the world has been changed more by *On the Origin of Species* than by any other book—at any rate since the time when Newton in his *Principia* propounded the theory of universal gravitation."

There may be family pride involved in this assertion, but it's fair. No secular text that I can think of changed the world's way of thinking more entirely; those few who still deny the theory of evolution are ostriches in sand. What the beak of the goldfinch and the Galapagos tortoise and a host of other instances suggested to Charles Darwin revised all previous assumptions about the nature and descent of man; we now more fully understand the ways in which our species has altered over time. This came about, of course, through years of rigorous observation and data collection, but it comes down to us in prose.

The tone is dispassionate, measured. He doesn't trumpet *God is Dead!* or *We come from Apes!* or even *Nature red in tooth and claw* (this last a quote from Alfred Lord Tennyson's "In Memoriam," 1850). Darwin's enemies might claim as much, accusing him of several sorts of apostasy, but the book itself is data-filled and calm. Its chapter titles tell the tale. They are, in stately succession: "Variation under Domestication," "Variation under Nature," "Struggle for Existence," "Natural Selection, or The Survival of the Fittest," "Laws of Variation," "Difficulties of the Theory," "Miscellaneous Objections to the Theory of Natural Selection," "Instinct," "Hybridism," "On the Imperfection of the Geological Record," "On the Geological Succession of Organic Beings," "Geographical Distribution," "Geographical Distribution (Continued)," "Mutual Affinities of Organic Beings: Morphology: Embryology: Rudimentary Organs," and "Recapitulation and Conclusion."

As he puts it in the opening beat of the final chapter:

Nothing at first can appear more difficult to believe than that the more complex organs and instincts have been perfected, not by means superior to, though analogous with, human reason, but by the accumulation of innumerable slight variations, each good for the individual possessor. Nevertheless, this difficulty, though appearing to our imagination insuperably great, cannot be considered real if we admit the following propositions, namely, that all parts of the organisation and instincts offer, at least, individual differences—that there is a struggle for existence leading to the preservation of profitable deviations of structure or instinct—and, lastly, that gradations in the state of perfection of each organ may have existed, each good of its kind. The truth of these propositions cannot, I think, be disputed.

Had his arguments been registered only in the Linnean Society, or the Royal Institution of Science, they might have, over time, had an equivalent effect. But because they were written and printed, they reached, almost on the instant, a wide and contentious and, by debate's end, credulous audience. *Why Writing Matters* can have no clearer piece of evidence than Charles Darwin's published work.

In the portrait painted by Édouard Manet (1868), Émile Zola holds a book in his left hand. He is well dressed, on a plush chair in front of a cluttered writing desk; his right hand rests on his right thigh, a few inches from his knee. The book he holds has illustrations; its title is the artist's signature, and much else in the painting is self-reflexive as well. On the desk stands a copy of Zola's pamphlet in praise of Manet, composed the year before. In his role as critic, the writer defended the painter from a charge of impropriety—of having attempted, in the French phrase, to "épater le bourgeois." The carefully attired sitter too was guilty of having "shocked the bourgeoisie"; in his novel *Thérèse Raquin* (1867) he described the adulterous, then murderous, affair of the title character and a would-be-painter who bore more than a passing resemblance to Zola's childhood friend, Paul Cézanne. This portrait is a thank-you note, a gift from one artist to another as a form of reciprocity for previous support.

On the dark wall behind the writer hang three additional works of art: the first a reproduction of Manet's own portrait of Olympia, the naked lady on a couch with a black neck-band and unabashed forward-facing stare. Behind the courtesan hangs a lithograph of a major painting by Diego Velázquez, commonly known as *Los Borrachos* or *The Drinkers* (1628). And there's a nineteenth-century Japanese print of a wrestler by Utagawa Kuniaki, as well as a Japanese screen behind the sitter, attesting to work in traditions admired by Manet.

These secondary figures look straight ahead; Zola himself is in profile, ignoring them, and gazing ruminatively out at empty space. His skin is white, his black beard trim, his forehead high, nose sharp. In some ways the image is more a testimonial to Manet's own interests than those of his subject; as the painter Odilon Redon observed in his salon revue (*La Gironde,* June 9, 1868), "It is rather a still life, so to speak, than the expression of a human being." Zola was reportedly less than elated by the portrait, keeping it in an antechamber of his home. In another man this might have been a self-effacing gesture, or an expression of humility; in the case of Émile Zola, self-effacement would rarely apply. His motto was instead, "If you ask me what I came into this life to do, I will tell you: I came to live out loud."

He made his name as a "muck-raking" critic and novelist, writing turn by turn of such societal ills as poverty, violence, and prostitution—attempting, in the twenty novels collectively known as the Rougon-Macquart series, to cover the full range of life in France's Second Empire. Outpacing even Victor Hugo, he became the period's best-selling novelist, writing of life in the provinces as well as the capital city. In *La Terre* he wrote of peasant life in Beauce, in *Germinal* of life in the mines, in *La Débacle* of life in the army. He was, if not the founder, a chief practitioner of the aesthetic strategy we now call naturalism, a melding of imagination and detailed reportage. Persuaded that behavior was influenced by environment, he sought meticulously to document the physical, sexual, fiscal, and social circumstance through which his characters moved.

Zola lived from 1840 to 1902, dying at his home in Paris of carbon monoxide poisoning from a perhaps suspiciously blocked chimney. More than a century after his death, however, he is better remembered for a brief essay than for his long novels—which, along with the encyclopedic project of Honoré de Balzac, *La Comédie Humaine,* feel a touch dutiful now. In some ways his work stands as a precursor of what we call "new journalism," with the author-commentator taking stage center as witness. But the role of the creative writer as reporter has been, in the contemporary moment, supplanted by other media. Journalism, television, movies, and the internet have replaced the novelist as the purveyor of *les nouvelles* or "news."

The newspaper article he published as "J'Accuse," however, still comes (in Hotspur's phrase from *Henry IV, Part I*) "current for an accusation." It was an open letter to the president of the French Republic, appearing in *L'Aurore* on January 13, 1898. "J'Accuse" caused a national uproar—a convulsion, even—in what became known as the "Dreyfus Affair." Few if any other articles in the history of journalism have had such galvanic effect.

Alfred Dreyfus, a Jew, was a captain of artillery in the French army. In 1894, French intelligence officers found evidence of someone in the army passing military secrets to the German embassy and thereby committing treason. With no direct proof of Dreyfus's guilt, but in an atmosphere of pervasive anti-Semitism, the career officer was arrested and by a secret court-martial sentenced to life imprisonment on Devil's Island off Guyana.

What followed was even less defensible. Two years later, a lieutenant-colonel, Georges Picquart, found evidence that yet another officer, Ferdinand Walsin Esterhazy, was the guilty party; he so informed his superiors. In the tradition-bound and bigoted higher reaches of the army, the decision was made to keep the original verdict intact, to shelter Esterhazy, and to forge a set of documents that would prove Dreyfus's guilt. Picquart, punitively assigned to duty in Africa, revealed what he had learned, and Senator Auguste Scheurer-Kestner argued in the Senate that Dreyfus was innocent, accusing Esterhazy. The government disallowed the new evidence, acquitted the actual traitor and, for good measure, prepared to court-martial Picquart.

Zola risked his reputation and career—even, it would seem, his life—by coming to Dreyfus's defense. His letter to Félix Faure, the president of the Republic, is a masterpiece of direct address and controlled invective; it's a sweeping condemnation of both process and result. "J'Accuse" is a remarkable document and model of its kind—though it may well be "one of a kind" in terms of its effectiveness.

The article opens with a flowery and flattering direct address: "Monsieur le Président: Will you permit me, in my gratitude for the so-generous welcome you one day gave me, to be concerned that your rightful glory and bright star, so happy until this moment, is now menaced by the most shameful and ineffaceable stain?" Further, the author asserts, "My duty is to speak, I do not want to be complicit." (My translation.) He then lays out in considerable detail the sequence of the accusations against Dreyfus, the conspiracy, the military cover-up, the collusion of the government, naming names. In specific as well as in general terms, and ending with the repeated phrase, "J'Accuse," Zola cites those who were in fact guilty and proclaims the innocence of the man who was convicted. He closes with seven paragraphs, each beginning "I accuse . . ." and moving from the particular (Generals Mercier, Billot, Boisdeffre, Gonse, etc.) to a categorical denunciation of handwriting experts, the department of war, and their press campaign. "Finally, I accuse the first council of war of having violated justice by condemning an accused man through evidence kept secret, and I accuse the second council of war of having, under orders, covered up that illegality and committing, in turn, the judicial crime of knowingly acquitting a guilty party." (My translation.)

His intention all along was to be sued for libel, so he could bring to light the newly available facts. On February 7, 1898, he was brought to trial and on February 23 convicted and removed from the Legion of Honor. Rather than serve a prison term, the writer fled to England—much the way that Victor Hugo, earlier, had moved to the island of Guernsey in opposition to the rule of Napoleon III.

Yet time was on his side. Whereas Marx and Engels had a general audience in mind with *The Communist Manifesto,* Zola in "J'Accuse" confronted the specific figure of the president of the Republic and, by extension, the government of France. Together, the Catholic Church, the military hierarchy, and the whole entrenched apparatus of anti-Semitism were at length defeated in a pitched battle dividing the nation (less bloody than, though reminiscent of, the argument over the Fugitive Slave Act and the ensuing Civil War). In 1906, Captain Alfred Dreyfus was completely exonerated by the French Supreme Court. By then his champion was dead but, as Zola had written, "The truth is on the march."

❧

Of *Lady Chatterley's Lover,* there's something personal to say. I was a little boy enthralled by reading, and one of the books on our library shelves was a slim gray volume, its spine stamped with that name. I had heard of it, of course, and couldn't wait for the chance to abscond to my room with the forbidden treasure; one afternoon, when my parents were elsewhere, I grabbed it and hurried upstairs. Avidly, I read what turned out to be a brief discourse on social conditions in a British mining town, its emphasis on class distinctions and on horticulture. There was some sort of disagreement between a wife and husband; there was a gardener called Mellors and a conspiracy of silence when he and Lady Chatterley spent time together alone. After tea, or in the garden, their behavior on the page went blank. A redacted document shows the reader what has been removed; this one showed a profusion of ellipses and white space . . .

What my mother or father had purchased in London—which is why it sat so visibly available for selection from the shelf—was the altogether expurgated edition of the novel, which would not be cleared for sale in its full naked glory for more than thirty years. The landmark decision of November 2, 1960, that this was art, not pornography, roughly doubled the length of the novel, which soon became a best-seller and made D. H. Lawrence (1885–1930) famous. From *John Thomas and Lady Jane,* the *ur-*text published in 1927, to the finished book published in Italy next year, then in 1929 in Australia and France—then finally to the trial in England under the Obscenity Law of 1959, where the verdict was "not guilty" and the Penguin edition soon sold three million copies—a long odyssey from censorship to free expression filled in those ellipses and blanks. Words like "fuck" and "cunt" were now permitted, though not in the version I'd read.

Much the same would happen to two other acknowledged modernist classics: James Joyce's *Ulysses* and Vladimir Nabokov's *Lolita.* I won't go into chapter and verse but the trajectory of those titles is similar: Works produced in the service of art and idiosyncratic expressiveness run afoul of censorship laws. After a protracted wrangle, they are cleared for publication and make their author (or, in the case of Joyce, their author's estate) rich. There has always been pornography, always erotica and "forbidden" acts portrayed in language and lines on the page, but the public, not private, availability of such books is relatively recent. Now, as Cole Porter put it in his rhyme about a glimpse of shocking stocking, "Anything Goes."

What Lawrence was after was more than shock value, of course. His was a proselytizer's zeal, a preacher-reformer's message. And what he wished to see reformed was the hidebound propriety of English middle- and upper-class behavior; with its stiff upper lip and buttoned-down lust, those buttons down well past the crotch. Like much else in his voluminous oeuvre, there's high-pitched insistence here; we must pay attention to and not repress the animal urges within us, says Lawrence, because those instincts are a component part of what it means to be human. Vitality abounds in nature, not industrial society, and the repressive force of the latter makes social and sexual rebellion more urgent. Necessary, even, if we are not to wither up and die. "A woman has to live her life, or repent not having lived it." This is a song he sang throughout his productive career.

A few more quotes from *Lady Chatterley's Lover* will suffice to remind the reader of Lawrence's position:

> Obscenity only comes in when the mind despises and fears the body, and the body hates and resists the mind.

> Never was an age more sentimental, more devoid of real feeling, more exaggerated in false feeling, than our own.

> For a moment he was still inside her, turgid there and quivering. Then as he began to move, in the sudden helpless orgasm, there awoke in her new strange thrills rippling inside her. Rippling, rippling, rippling, like a flapping overlapping of soft flames, soft as feathers, running to points of brilliance, exquisite and melting her all molten inside. It was like bells rippling up and up to a culmination. She lay unconscious of the wild little cries she uttered at the last.

Or, more simply, "We fucked a flame into being."

All this feels a bit dated now, and it's not easy to remember how daring it once seemed. The battle has been won. What Lawrence (or his American counterpart, Henry Miller) fought for in their novels and non-fiction works was a freedom of expression and unfettered access to desire. To be "in touch with one's feelings" was to live authentically, and the more so if those feelings were made manifest in sex. The serial couplings of lady and gardener were intended to—and did—stand for the breaking down of barriers, both physical and mental: a set of barriers imposed by those behavior patterns the novelist would rail against and flout. For David Herbert Lawrence, the frail son of a coal miner in Nottinghamshire, England, to have run off with the previously married Frieda von Richthofen, and to have lived with her in Italy, then Mexico, New Mexico, and France was to have surpassed expectation and transgressed societal boundaries in almost equal measure. He was over-rhapsodic and wordy, perhaps, but an authentic renegade, and his preachment was applauded by the sexual and social liberation movements of the 1960s and 1970s. If Lawrence was a prophet, then his central text is *Lady Chatterley's Lover,* and the gospel has been preached.

A less well known and smaller effort, *The Man Who Died,* does much the same. In that novella, Lawrence resurrects (though never overtly names) the figure of Jesus come down from the cross. At the climactic moment, after a slow and painful rebirth—his wounds and deathly pallor are described at length—under the ministrations of a serving woman, the man who died cries "I am risen." This double entendre and not-so-subtle sexual reference (his original working title had been *The Escaped Cock*) attempts to do for Christian doctrine what *Chatterley* did for the world of the flesh: the profane made sacred, the sacred made profane.

It's possible that societal mores would have changed without his novel, probable it was a symptom as well as a transforming agent of the time. But here's one final example of a text that made a difference, of a thing written that *mattered*. Neither *Uncle Tom's Cabin* nor *Lady Chatterley's Lover* are untrammeled in their excellence as fictions; neither qualifies—at least in this reader's opinion—as a triumph of the form. But both were major agents of change. The two societal struggles—one for liberation of the slaves, one for behavioral freedom—found creative documents to press into public service as foot soldiers in the fight. H. B. Stowe and D. H. Lawrence, by virtue of their writings, changed the way their readers viewed and acted in the world—no small thing to have accomplished with a piece of prose.

This well may be what Shelley meant by "unacknowledged legislators"; none of these authors ran for office, none was of the ruling class or able to command attention *without* the written word. But because of the power of language and an attentive readership, the world they left behind them was not the one they entered. Uncle Tom and Lady Chatterley are imagined creatures, both, yet both of them took flight beyond the page.

In the chapters that follow I plan to be both more private and present-tense in focus, as if the subtext of the text might read, "Why Writing Matters to Me." I want to write of my students, the nature of apprenticeship, and the learning curve that writing workshops provide. I plan to track the distance between an act of imitation and that of originality, how the two seeming opposites are apposite in nature, and how each and all of us depend on mimesis—a conscious copying of what went before. This will entail a discussion of influence, plagiarism, pseudonyms, of the various ways that writing in a variety of rhetorics can shift the way we see. The topic is a large one, and no single volume—no matter how wide ranging—can hope to be encyclopedic; I make no such claim and have no such intention. Better to admit to begin with that this is a surface-scratch, and that all-inclusiveness is beyond these pages' scope. The five texts in this chapter each had a major impact; five hundred others did too.

4 true or false

I want to tell three stories. In order to preserve the privacy of the people here described, I've changed a very few details and omitted proper names, but the storylines themselves are based upon flat fact. In each case the issue of plagiarism is the problem posed. And in each case, long years later, I'm haunted by the principals—the principles—involved.

The first takes place in Bennington College, Vermont, in 1972. I offered an Advanced Prose Fiction Workshop, for which there were many more applicants than places at table, and I therefore asked for writing samples from those who hoped to enroll. Young writers at Bennington—soon to include such notables as Bret Easton Ellis and Donna Tartt—had a sense of being singled out and engaged in a high calling. The dozen I selected seemed glad and proud and nervous in nearly equal measure to come to our three-hour class. We met on Wednesday mornings to talk about the craft, submitting work in progress; the discussions were lively and the participants engaged. Every creative writing workshop has its own dynamic; this one soon enough established a shared sense of purpose, with real talent in the room.

One young man—let's call him X—was the exception. He seemed half asleep and wholly inattentive; when it came time to discuss his own proffered work he roused himself, a little, but couldn't explain his artistic choices and bungled his characters' names. Soon, X started skipping class—a major infraction in that context, and one I had announced I'd be unwilling to forgive. In what seemed to me a clear attempt to curry favor, he came to my office and declared he'd seen Mick Jagger over the previous weekend in New York: Mick sent regards. As it happens, I did know a number of popular music stars, but Jagger was not one of them, and this put me on my guard; X might have known of my association with others in the performance world, but why would he lie? I made inquiries.

The boy was rich. He came from the West Coast; his father was a power broker in the entertainment industry, and he had many—let's call them—weaknesses of personal behavior. He did drugs. He sold them to other students or as an act of largesse gave the drugs away. He liked to chain his girlfriends to their dormitory beds, and if they complained he used the chains to beat them into something like submission. He kept guns. Bennington was a permissive place, and the early 1970s were years of frank experimentation, but X went beyond the pale. If not a full-fledged psychopath, he was certainly a sociopath, and by his sophomore year he'd made large local waves. More than once he had been summoned to explain himself before the Student Judicial Committee—a committee, as the name suggests, whose charge was to pronounce upon infraction of the rules.

There were few rules. He proved agile in his own defense: the drugs were free, the girls had *asked* for bondage, he was a collector, and the pistols and rifles in his possession were not used. He cited the Second Amendment; the sex had been consensual; cocaine was common currency; and others were involved. Much of his activity came down to "He said/she said," and X had the wherewithal to be litigious if expelled. So though the college imposed a form of probation upon him, he remained on campus and sometimes came to class.

All through the fall, however, he failed to provide prose fiction other than the stories with which he had applied, and when I warned him he'd not pass the course he shrugged and turned away. A few dull pages trickled in. Then, near the end of the year, his roommate Y came to my office and said he'd like to enroll in the Prose Fiction Workshop scheduled for next semester. I told him what I told all applicants, that he should show me a sample of prose, and I'd make a decision and post the list of those accepted for the spring. He said he couldn't do that, and I asked him why. Y said I'd seen his stories; they were brought to class by X. I asked him to explain, and he said he loved prose fiction and was trying hard to improve on his own, but every time he wrote a page his roommate Xeroxed it and submitted it for workshop—which was why, not incidentally, X couldn't discuss the motivation of his characters or even remember their names.

We threw X out of Bennington on the charge of plagiarism. That was the cardinal offense, the one rule he could not flout. Drug-dealing, guns, and rape did not engender expulsion, but the high crime of academe—copying the work of others—was unforgivable. All these decades later (X made headlines next year for taking out a contract on his parents, hoping for an early inheritance, but the "hit man" turned him in; Y never did become a writer, since his prose was second-rate), I think of plagiarism as the line you cannot cross. Abandon all hope, ye who copy here.

The second such instance arose in Ann Arbor at the turn of the millennium. At the University of Michigan, I served as chair of the Hopwood Awards Committee: a prize-giving entity that by tradition confers both cash and cachet on its award recipients. The contest—with previous winners such as Mary Gaitskill, Lawrence Kasdan, Arthur Miller, and Marge Piercy—was established in the early 1930s, with substantial funds. The successful poets, prose writers, essayists, screenwriters, and playwrights are selected by a process ensuring anonymity; there are stringent rules. Those who enter the Hopwood competition do so under a pseudonym; their work is judged by strangers, not members of the local faculty, and the selection process is therefore double-blind. The chair of the Hopwood Committee—I held that post for nearly thirty years—honors writing students in a formal ceremony in late April; the hall is full. When their names are announced, the winners come on stage to loud rounds of applause.

Among the honorees in the several categories on that April afternoon, a young woman won the graduate poetry contest; I handed the student—let's call her A—an envelope containing a check and a citation for the prize. Next day another poet came to see me in my office, on the verge of tears. I asked B what the trouble was, and she said her own losing entry had been plagiarized, that she and A shared a workshop, and the victorious Hopwood manuscript was based upon her work. I asked for evidence. We had the award-winning poems on file, and since B furnished her own original drafts, we were able to compare.

Indeed there were marked similarities with the "losing" student's work. It was not a word-for-word equivalence but what I've been calling here a variation on a theme, and   to my eye and ear, at least—the winning manuscript was an improvement on the original. In Bennington I'd conducted the prose fiction workshop where problems arose; at Michigan another faculty member was responsible for the poetry class, and I called her in and asked for her opinion. On the merits of the actual verse, we agreed. I asked for the written opinions of several other poets; they concurred: there were indeed verbal echoes, but contestant A deserved the prize.

There remained the thorny problem of the complainant's outrage; she told me she felt violated, robbed. In the group dynamic of the graduate poetry workshop, each student passed out samples of his or her work for close classroom analysis; A therefore had copies of B's poems, and B insisted that her ideas and emotions—indeed, her whole artistic enterprise—had been stolen and reconfigured by her colleague in the class. Among the rules and regulations for the Hopwood contest is very specific language about plagiarism and, in the larger sense, originality; the work cannot have been previously published; it cannot be an adaptation of the work of others or a translation or revision of some secondary text.

The committee met. We agreed that A had adapted the poetry of B and rescinded the award. Now it was A's turn to be outraged and to lodge a protest; she demanded we reconsider the decision and restore her prize. (Interestingly, neither of the poets made any mention of the money involved; all that seemed to matter was the Hopwood award itself.) I had hoped to keep the process private and informal, but soon enough the apparatus of university bureaucracy—its committees of inquiry, its lawyers and a board of appeals—was involved. Plagiarism is a mortal not a venial sin in the academy, and A's graduation was at stake.

The defendant's argument was, in effect, culture based. She was of mixed ancestry, part Japanese, part Hawaiian, and accustomed to collective utterance; her whole early education had consisted of shared and repeated stories; it was a compliment, not insult, to another author if you referred to their work. She freely admitted that B's poetry, discussed in their classroom sessions, had struck a chord, enriching her own poems by association. But she hotly denied any intention of theft. If you write a love sonnet, she argued, or a description of mountains and clouds, can you be accused of illegal borrowing from previous verse about romance or nature? If you use a simile that Milton or Middleton used before, is it an act of plagiarism or simply a tip of the cap? The whole point of a creative writing workshop, A said, is that you work together with your cohort; why was she being singled out—discriminated against, really—for having learned from what a colleague wrote some months before and then producing her own version of the text?

Many years later (A has become a much-published poet; not so, to my knowledge, has B), I can neither remember the verdict we reached nor the formal disposition of the suit. It was full of legal niceties, a kind of willed institutional avoidance, and unlike the verdict reached at Bennington (that the plagiarist must be expelled), the "copyist" stayed on. Her claim remains with me, moreover, as a nuanced one, an assertion of the right to borrow, and not to call such borrowings a theft.

The third case is an instance in which I myself was charged. In 2006 I published a novel called *Spring and Fall* and dedicated it to my long-standing agent Gail Hochman. Not so loosely patterned on Shakespeare's *The Winter's Tale,* it tracked the early affair and separation of a couple (based on Leontes and Hermione) who meet again forty years later. Lawrence, a music-loving architect, has health issues: trouble with his heart. Hermia's child, Patricia (based on Perdita in Shakespeare's play), disappears and, at the end of the action, returns. The book sold some copies, earned a respectful review or two, and soon went the way of all less-than-best-sellers, disappearing from the shelf.

But it had been noticed by a woman in Chicago who filed suit for plagiarism of her own unpublished novel, which she argued I had copied. Her protagonist played the saxophone; his lover had a hysterectomy, and these two issues—the matter of music, the matter of health—seemed sufficiently akin to her so she assumed I must have read her manuscript. This would have been a nuisance suit, thrown out of court summarily, but for a pair of mitigating factors. First, she was indigent, representing herself against a well-heeled corporation (Warner Books was then my publisher), and the law does make provisions to shield and assist the poor. Second, she'd sent her own manuscript to the Brandt & Hochman Agency in the hope of representation; she had been refused.

As time wore on, I read her argument: handwritten, fairly percolating with insanity. She'd not in fact read *Spring and Fall* but a review of it in the *Chicago Tribune,* and that had been enough. It was clear as clear could be, she wrote, that Gail Hochman saw the value of her novel and stole the idea and gave it to me, a recognized author, to copy out in language of my own. I thought this laughable but was told by Warner Books it was no laughing matter; by contract they assumed the first legal costs, though the process was an elaborate one and soon enough the limits of their liability would be reached. My agent and I would shoulder the ensuing expense of a lawsuit, and it would be large. Did I have any evidence to defend myself against the charge of plagiarism; what sources had I used? Shakespeare's late romance was admittedly in the public domain, but how could I prove that my lovers were not related to—indeed stolen from—hers?

Fortunately, I'd signed the contract for the novel *before* the complainant's unpublished manuscript reached the desk of and was rejected by my dedicatee; we did have proof of the dates. There was no logical way her work in progress could have influenced my book. The lawsuit was withdrawn. But in its own improbable fashion it too raised the matter of originality and borrowing; if a character plays an instrument and falls in love, why could he not be patterned on every character since Orpheus, and if you somehow own the copyright of the word "Orpheus" why should you not file claim? As X had learned at Bennington, plagiarism is a mighty charge, not easy to dismiss. Too, I found myself thinking about A and B, their outrage many years before; the issue is a vexed one, and it won't go away.

In terms of that vexed issue and formal full disclosure, I should acknowledge a phrase in the first sentence of two paragraphs previous. "Fairly percolating with insanity" is an unattributed quotation from a short story by Charles Baxter, "Fenstad's Mother." There the author has a character "percolating slightly with insanity" in an all-night restaurant called Country Bob's. That phrase stayed with me for years.

My substitution for the original adverb was, however, inadvertent. I used it to describe the woman's written complaint, and only when I looked at his story again did I recognize I had misremembered Baxter's description as "fairly percolating with insanity," not "percolating slightly . . ." This happens, I think, often. We overhear a snatch of speech and later on repeat it; we find an expression compelling and borrow it for use. My recollection, inaccurate though it may be, suggests I'd come to make the original four words part of a collective memory, "appropriating" another author's fine phrase as my own. Therefore my thanks but no quotes . . .

By contrast the last line of the first story here recounted—"Abandon all hope, ye who copy here"—is a direct reference to the words above the Gates of Hell: "Abandon all hope, ye who enter here." This is the sort of borrowing all writers traffic in, and the line from Dante Alighieri has become part of the public domain; it would defeat the point of paraphrase to cite its original source. In Charles Baxter's case the reference was and is sufficiently personal to merit a citation. But when a phrase has fully entered into our shared lexicon, it would be pedantic to identify its origin in speech.

So as not to be again accused of theft, let me here cite the source of the definition of the word *plagiarism* from the World Wide Web (Dictionary.com):

> Plagiarism: noun
>
> 1. An act or instance of using or closely imitating the language and thoughts of another author without authorization and the representation of that author's work as one's own, as by not crediting the original author.
>
> Synonyms: appropriation; infringement; piracy, counterfeiting; theft; borrowing; cribbing; passing off.
>
> 2. A piece of writing or other work reflecting such unauthorized use or imitation.

Here is the word's origin:

> n. 1620's, from—ism + plagiary (n.) "plagiarist, literary thief" (1590's) from Latin plagiarius, "kidnapper, seducer, plunderer, one

who kidnaps the child or slave of another," used by Martial in the sense of "literary thief," from plagiare "to kidnap," plagium, "kidnapping" from plaga, "snare, hunting net . . ."

Textbooks and MLA manuals are full of much more elaborate definitions of plagiarism and instructions on how to avoid it. Even in a period of false report and baseless rumor—so prevalent in print today—there's no more glaring error than the failure to cite quotations. The work of predecessors is a necessary precondition of one's own original work. Footnotes and full documentation are an integral component of any published article, and every dissertation must track and formally acknowledge its primary and secondary source material. Such synonyms as *infringement, piracy, counterfeiting, theft* all indicate the legal risks of plagiarism and—in order to avoid the charge itself—strict standards of behavior that the scholar must accept.

Nor does this system apply to the apprentice only; professional practitioners are equally at risk. Off the top of my head I can think of several recent accusations of "piracy" by prominent authors: Alex Haley in *Roots*, John Gardner in his biography of Chaucer, Doris Kearns Goodwin in *The Fitzgeralds and the Kennedys,* Jill Abramson in *Merchants of Truth*. There are many more. Stephen Ambrose, to take just one additional example, fell afoul of the same charge: certain paragraphs in his best-selling books had been closely patterned on the prose of less celebrated accounts. In each case the writer claimed in self-defense that the process of note-taking was a complicated one. Their research was extensive, sometimes conducted by others; there had been nothing intentional about the error of omission; after years and years of using a phrase they could not fully recollect or feel the need to cite a long-forgotten source. If you consult an old file folder and find a line you've copied out, must you provide the citation or exhume the original quote?

The majority of such instances come in the non-fiction mode; it's harder to accuse an author of poetry or fiction of unlawful borrowing. Jerzy Kosinski (of *The Painted Bird* and *Being There*) *was* charged with unacknowledged appropriation of the work of Polish predecessors; his suicide, in 1991, is thought in part to have resulted from that charge. Malcolm Lowry's *Ultramarine* is chock-a-block with passages from Nordahl Grieg's *Blue Voyage* and fear on the young author's part that he would be accused. T. S. Eliot's seminal poem "The Waste Land" is built on borrowings, but because of his footnotes and citations the writer seemed to be assessing a cultural condition ("these fragments I have shored against my ruins") and not committing theft. Remember his assertion that "Immature poets borrow, mature poets steal," and the aesthetic of "The Waste Land" can be in part explained.

This sort of retroactive homage seems habitual. But familiar, too, is the way we dismiss old models, whether they be books we read as children, or movies once loved that make us cringe when watched a second time. The stages of age entail "outgrowing" youthful modes of expression the way we have outgrown old attitudes and clothes.

Two major critical studies—Walter Jackson Bate's *The Burden of the Past* (1970) and Harold Bloom's *The Anxiety of Influence* (1973)—describe the nexus, for writers, of a tradition embraced and thereafter rejected. We all remember something learned in grade school or high school or college that has stayed with us as instruction; we improve our skills by copying and then attempting to say (or write, or draw, or dance) something original. It's the time-honored sequence of apprenticeship: you spend years under someone's tutelage (present or distant, in the flesh or on the page), then set out on your own.

When I wrote, near the start of Chapter 2, that "all writers read all the time," I meant to suggest we're suggestible; if you admire the work of long-dead practitioners or wish to emulate a living artist it's hard not to borrow at least a small component of their craft. Those constituent parts—this one's use of metaphor, that one's delight in the four-letter word, that one's ear for dialogue and this one's deployment of brand names—will sooner or later add up to a whole, and with luck a signature. Put it another way: take a pinch of A, a dab of B, a whiff of C, and stir well through the alphabet soup until you produce your own stew. At the end of an apprenticeship, you should be able both to emulate your masters and to leave their work behind. The model here again is that of Dante, who—in the third part of his journey—departs from his guide, Virgil, walking on alone. To watch the young writer discover their own particular voice is to listen to them practice scales and start out often croakingly until they grow full-throated. For once we recognize a predecessor and acknowledge influence, it begins to wane. This is an alchemical process—a pattern of growth and transformation—that every teacher witnesses and all students know.

There have been famous instances of forgery in print. This seems a different problem, more a matter of false representation than plagiarism, but akin: the writer passes off her or his own work as the work of others. The youthful Thomas Chatterton (1752–1770)—whom Wordsworth called "that marvellous boy"—was able for a time to publish the poetry of "Thomas Rowley," an imaginary fifteenth-century monk whose work he himself composed. Fatherless and raised in poverty, the young man was unable to earn a living with his language skills. Studious but ill-connected, and without a patron, he received mere shillings for his articles and verse.

Three days after telling a friend "I have been at war with the grave for some time now," Chatterton killed himself. Having torn up the manuscript pages on which he was fruitlessly laboring, he swallowed arsenic in a London attic. Now there's a plaque on the office building (39 Brooke Street, Holborn) that has replaced the boarding house; it bears the inscription:

In a House on this Site
Thomas Chatterton
Died
24 August, 1770

As befits the high romantic mode, a young and brilliant suicide—he was not yet eighteen—has become a paradigm of selfless devotion to art. Chatterton's doomed search for recognition and the scattered fragments of his verse gave rise to a posthumous legend. William Wordsworth, as we have seen, "thought of Chatterton, the marvellous Boy / the Sleepless Soul that perished in his pride." Percy Bysshe Shelley wrote of the poet in "Adonais,"

John Keats inscribed "Endymion" "To the memory of Thomas Chatterton"; the French poet Alfred de Vigny wrote a play titled *Chatterton,* and Peter Ackroyd published a novel of the same name. Several songs and madrigals describe his fate; the Italian composer Ruggiero Leoncavallo, the German Matthias Pintscher, and the Australian Matthew Dewey each produced an opera with the poet as protagonist. The English painter Henry Walls memorialized him in *The Death of Chatterton* (1856) now hanging in London's Tate Britain gallery, and there's a collection of "Chattertoniana" in The British Museum. Unacknowledged during his lifetime, he's much honored after death.

Vincent van Gogh is a roughly equivalent figure in the visual arts. Alive, he was unable to sell paintings that now sell for millions of dollars, and his fierce focus on his work today seems inspirational, though it was then deemed insane. John Keats too died young, though not a suicide. For his grave he chose the phrase "Here lies one whose name is writ in water." That proved untrue. But both these celebrated artists were pursuing their own creative vision, not cutting or trimming that vision in order to accommodate the marketplace. It would take years for the viewing and reading public to recognize the value of the art produced; there's nothing derivative here. It's routinely the case that innovative artistic expression is met—to begin with—by a blank stare. As with the work of the aging Beethoven, Rembrandt, or Monet, the early expressive masterworks of such artists as Van Gogh or Keats came "before their time."

"Thomas Rowley" is a different proposition. Thomas Chatterton, or so it seems, elected conscious deception in the attempt to make a living from the work of words. He killed himself while still a teenager, so it's at best conjectural to imagine what his poems would have looked like had he continued to write. (This holds true, as well, for the visionary French poet Arthur Rimbaud, who ceased to compose at nineteen.) It seems unlikely, though not impossible, that Chatterton would have deployed the language of the fifteenth century for the rest of his writing career; more likely, had he found an audience, he would have done so under his own name and using his own voice. Extant fragments seem a *cri de coeur* in the hope of funds.

At times the desire for profit comes more nakedly stage center. There are several versions of the counterfeiter's trade—as in the fraud of the *Autobiography of Howard Hughes* by Clifford Irving (1972), *The Hitler Diaries* (1983), and *A Million Little Pieces* by James Frey (2003). In the first instance the "ghostwriter" banked on the famously reclusive nature of his subject to invent a life; in the second "historical" text the act of forgery was total; in the third the author embellished his own history in order to make it more lurid and therefore commercial as a book. These examples have less to do with imitation than authenticity, so I shall leave them unexamined—but in each instance the author's false representation raises the issue of legitimate ownership; how does one stake one's claim?

The case of "Ossian" is a case in point. The Scottish poet James Macpherson (1736–1796) announced he had discovered a trove of ancient fragments dealing with the legendary hero Finn Mac-

Cool. "Oisin" or "Ossian" was said to have been the hero's son, and his translated verse gained wide international currency. He was compared to and considered the equal of Homer: a blind bard singing the story of Fingal (or Fionnghall, "the white stranger") in Great Britain's early dark ages: a verbal treasure reclaimed. Soon enough the unknown artist became a cultural avatar and a best-selling one. Napoleon and Diderot considered him a master; so did Thomas Jefferson, who planned to study Gaelic so as to read the poems in their original tongue. The tales of love and battle and grief and joy were everywhere applauded.

In 1760 Macpherson first published *Fragments of Ancient Poetry, Collected in the Highlands of Scotland, and Translated from the Gaelic or Erse Language.* The next year he claimed to find an epic on the subject of Fingal, and there was a collected edition of *The Works of Ossian* in 1765. Macpherson argued, in his prefatory note, that his publisher had insisted on the English language—saying there was no market for the work except in English. In short order, however, the poems were translated into French and German and many other languages (Italian, Swedish, Danish, Russian, Dutch among them). The vogue of picturesque ruins and wandering minstrels with plucked harps enlarged. The blind bard engendered a cult. Ossian was celebrated by painters and composers; at his death his "translator" received that highest of posthumous accolades: a burial in Westminster Abbey.

But it was all a fake. Some doubted the work from the start. Samuel Johnson, among others, found both the poetry and poet unsound, calling Macpherson "a mountebank, a liar and a fraud." Further, he dismissed the language, asserting that many men, women, and children could have composed these "forgeries." More temperate scholars disagreed as to the legitimacy of sources—some saying it was a compilation of folk tales and oral fragments, others that the whole text was invented by Macpherson. Committees were convened to establish authenticity; study after study disputed or defended Ossian's art. By now the notion of a blind bard in the Scottish hills singing songs that rivaled Homer's has been discredited, but this leaves unanswered the question of the text itself; why should Fingal have been so much admired when considered "true," reviled when read as "false"?

A subset of this problem has to do with pseudonyms. Some established authors use pen names for their secondary productions; Joyce Carol Oates and John Banville, for example, distinguish their "serious" efforts from their "entertainments" by retaining their own names for the former and, in the latter instance, using pseudonyms. This distinction had been drawn by Graham Greene, though he signed his "entertainments" with his own actual name. Georges Simenon wrote hundreds of novels and, it would appear, used twenty-seven pseudonyms for work he considered of minor importance. This is automatic writing, almost, as though the author were a conduit for language he did not so much arrange as transcribe. As with the sheer volume of music produced by Mozart or Bach, it's hard to imagine a moment when the artist paused to revisit or even consciously "compose" his prose. The poets William Butler Yeats and, more recently, James Merrill said they took dictation at certain stages of their careers, though they continued to claim authorship under their own names.

Others use a *nom de plume*. For years the true identity of Pauline Réage, the author of the scandalous *Story of O.,* was undiscovered. For years the true identity of the best-selling Italian author, Elena Ferrante, has remained open to question. The great English novelist who published as George Eliot was in fact Marianne Evans, who feared her work would be taken less seriously if the public knew its author was a woman. The same holds true for George Sand—whose actual name was Amantine-Lucile-Aurore Dupin. The French satirist François Rabelais brought his work out under the anagrammatic pseudonym "Alcofribas Nasier." The poet known as H. D. (1886–1961) was Hilda Doolittle; "Saki" was the chosen name of the short-story writer H. H. Munro (1870–1916). In 1945, Cyril Connolly published *The Unquiet Grave* as "Palinurus," and the list goes on.

Were I to reissue my own last novel *The Years* (2015) under someone else's name, could that be construed as a plagiarism of Delbanco's work? F. Scott Fitzgerald ascribed the epigraph of *The Great Gatsby* to the fictitious poet Thomas Parke D'Invilliers, because his quatrain so perfectly suited the novel it introduced. In fact he composed it himself:

> Then wear the gold hat, if that will move her;
> If you can bounce high, bounce for her too.
> Till she cry, "Lover, gold-hatted, high-bouncing lover
>   I must have you."

Would *The Years* be importantly altered if its title page displayed some pseudonym for its original author? Does the poem lose its currency because incorrectly ascribed? The answers to these questions are both no. But the question of ascription remains a cogent one; if a rose were called "skunk cabbage," would it smell as sweet?

⤱

The artist Katsushika Hokusai (1760–1849) is said to have said of his painting: "At seventy-three I learned a little about the real structure of animals, plants, birds, fishes and insects. Consequently when I am eighty I'll have made more progress. At ninety I'll have penetrated the mystery of things. At a hundred I shall have reached something marvelous, but when I am a hundred and ten everything I do, the smallest dot, will be alive."

These lines come to us in translation, and his most famous pronouncement, that he was "An old man mad about painting" has also been translated as "An old man mad with painting." But whether the word is "about" or "with," the sentiment holds just as true for the art of writing. A century later, Ford Madox Ford (1873–1939) called himself "An old man mad about writing," with a *salaam* to Hokusai. An editor and poet, memoirist and travel writer, Ford produced such major fictions as *The Good Soldier, The Fifth Queen* trilogy, and the tetralogy *Parade's End*. English-born, the author came from a German family (his original surname was Hueffer) and died in Deauville, France; he composed the last of his dozens of volumes in the small town of Olivet, Michigan.

Ford's final and staggeringly ambitious work is called *The March of Literature*. Published in America in 1938, it tackles subjects as ancient as "The Hebrews in Bondage," "Xenophon Lives the Anabasis," "Kau-Tsu Founds the Tang Dynasty," "The Vulgate and the *Versio Recepta,*" then moves through "The Orlando Furioso of Ariosto," "Donne's Impatience," "The Procuress Celestina," "The Picaresque Novel," "Lazarillo de Tormes," and closes with such relatively modern topics as "The Enigmatic Mr. Dickens," and "Balzac's Tinny Rhythm." By page 825, "We come then to Flaubert, Henry James and Joseph Conrad."

If it be true that "In the beginning was the word," it's also true that "In my end is my beginning." For Ford Madox Ford in *The March of Literature,* and for countless other adepts of his lifelong project, it's not so much a matter of completion as continuation. In this regard, apprenticeship is the time-honored mode of study that absorbs the work of others till it becomes one's own. And what was past is prologue: writing and reading march on.

5 strategies in prose

What follows is the syllabus for a course I called "Strategies in Prose" and taught often over the years. I first offered it at Bennington College in the early 1980s, then altered and refined it at the University of Michigan; I taught it in workshops from New York to San Francisco till it became a signature of sorts. At both the graduate and undergraduate level, the work produced was notable, and this chapter contains examples thereof. It's my contention that the work of imitation allowed these writing students to "check ego at the door," and that their ensuing work did profit from what I called apprenticeship. (Some of the language in the syllabus echoes—or, more accurately, prefigures—some of the argument in Chapter 2.) The prose hereafter reproduced is by young writers no longer quite so young; each of them is now a published author.

The novelists in this course syllabus are mannerists, in the sense that their prose is highly stylized and, to a degree, idiosyncratic. I could have picked another half-dozen recent major writers, from Alice Munro to William Trevor, whose prose style is less manifestly theirs and theirs alone. But the point of this procedure (and the exercise of imitation techniques) was and is to highlight how a book and its component parts—a sentence, a paragraph, a chapter—is by its author built.

STRATEGIES IN PROSE

This course will deal, in two-week discussion segments and in the following sequence, with these six novels:

A FAREWELL TO ARMS, ERNEST HEMINGWAY
THE GOOD SOLDIER, FORD MADOX FORD
TO THE LIGHTHOUSE, VIRGINIA WOOLF
AS I LAY DYING, WILLIAM FAULKNER
A PORTRAIT OF THE ARTIST AS A YOUNG MAN,
JAMES JOYCE
UNDER THE VOLCANO, MALCOLM LOWRY

Classroom discussion will also deal with the exercises that follow. There are some explanatory remarks as to those exercises on the last page, but here I want to introduce some general notions. I'd like to take as model for this course that of the medieval guild, and the assumption is we're all apprenticed to a trade. In this instance, we have the enduring achievements of six masterful authors to emulate and, ideally, by December we'll receive our walking/ working papers. It's an approximate model only, and not one to be over-scrupulous about, but there are several attributes thereof to keep in mind.

First, the whole impulse towards "self-expression" is a recent and possibly aberrant one in art. Legions of accomplished writers found nothing shameful in prescribed or proscribed subjects, or in eschewing the first-person pronoun. Though you come prepared to write your own life's story, or that of the St. Jago's monkey your great-uncle trained while plying the Sargasso Sea, have patience for a season, please; that's not our purpose here.

Neither is "signature" important. The bulk of our literature's triumphs have been collective or anonymous; who can identify the authors of the Bible, the Ramayana, or *Beowulf*? More importantly, who cares? The *Iliad* and *Odyssey* are by an unknown bard—as are, for all practical purposes, the plays of William Shakespeare. This is not to say that these works don't display personality—the reverse is more nearly true—but rather that the cult of personality should fade. It too is recent and, I think, aberrant; it has nothing to do with the labor of writing as such.

So what I want to focus on is craft, the craft of our six exemplars (which will imply a special way of reading them) and some delimited problems they pose. Instead of asking what does Joyce mean, we'll talk of what means he deploys; instead of discussing Woolf as an incipient suicide, we'll talk of Mrs. Ramsay's death in a parenthesis. To attempt a comprehensive reading of any of these authors in our brief semester-span is foolish; to attempt to comprehend the way they marshal metaphor is possible, perhaps. The article of faith on which this course is based is that imitation is not merely sincere flattery, but also a good way to grow. And if any of us contrives to echo, in any of these exercises, those masterful tonalities these master-compositors sounded, then there'll be music indeed.

One final cautionary note. Since the whole thrust here is process, don't worry overmuch about result. It's better to attempt and fail than not to try at all. Thus ends my catechism.

PLAUSIBLE EXERCISES

1. Add a chapter to the middle of any of the books under discussion.

2. Rewrite the ending via (a) substitution of an alternative, (b) an epilogue that reverses the terms of the preceding action, or (c) an epilogue that amplifies—an additional character, letter in a bottle, note in a desk-drawer, etc.

3. Introduce a dialogue or incident that the author would and should have cut.

4. Deal with imagery à la the six stylistic prototypes—how Joyce treats water as opposed to Hemingway and Woolf; a horse in the six ways that they might describe it; dawn; dusk; a timepiece.

5. Social rank: deal with this substantive question in the six fashions.

6. Lovemaking:" ".

7. Death:" ".

8. Some theme or context that none of them confront, and do so in their terms. Medieval pageantry, space travel; Twitter or Facebook; explicit same-sex passion, etc.

9. Write a Lowry-like parody of Hemingway, a Faulknerian of Ford.

10. Dress a character in the six fashions; have them plant a garden or justify their preference in drink.

11. Rewrite a page; change nothing (change, I mean, nothing of substance but alter the style).

12. Rewrite the dinner party in *To the Lighthouse* as a Hemingway scene; rewrite a section of Lowry's book—perhaps the reunion of the Consul and Yvonne—in Dowell's voice; give us Lafe's courtship of Dewey Dell as though it took place in a Dublin pub.

13. Landscape. First provide an appropriate terrain and time of day and year for each of the six instances. Then reverse their terms so that Stephen visits Mexico, Mrs. Ramsay goes to the Italian front, Edward Ashburnham visits Leonora's American cousins, the Bundrens.

14. Dialogue. Let Stephen Daedalus discuss with Hugh Firmin the flaws in Ford; have Frederick Henry tell nurse Catherine (who is a

literature, not art, student as they row to Switzerland) his opinion of Faulkner.

15. Monologue. The protagonists introduce in retrospect their story to follow. One day after the fact, one year, ten years; from the grave.

16. Write a critical preface to any of the novels. From the author's point of view. "What I was after here," etc.

17. Pastiche: Create a scene in the six styles seriatim, but so it emerges as a single scene, not six.

18. Satire, or the alteration of tone: make Frederick Henry's plunge into the river a comedy, ditto with Cash and Darl's river crossing; make Nancy's repeated "Credo in unum Deum Omnipotentem" a lascivious line, not chaste.

19. Transposition: Turn an available monologue into dialogue and vice versa; shift point of view, so that the first person becomes the third, and vice versa; shift tense so the present becomes the past, the past the present, and so on.

20. Revision: Recast one of your own available short stories or poems into the six tones.

21. Reconfiguration: Employ an alternate form—set a dialogue as theater scene, a descriptive passage as sonnet, an expressed character-attitude as essay.

22. Write a critical monograph on some aspect of pure rhetoric in one or more of the authors under discussion: *explication de texte*.

23. Process: Take as your endpoint the closing passage of *A Farewell to Arms* or *A Portrait of the Artist as a Young Man*. Then work toward that model in numerous revisions until you reproduce it letter perfect.

24. Do the same with the opening passage of *The Good Soldier* or *Under the Volcano*. Start, I mean, with a version of that first paragraph and refine and rewrite it until you attain the actual printed thing.

25. Select an example in each of the books that strikes you as a paradigm of style, and defend.

26. " ", then attack.

27. Change character color; make Jewel a Native American or Rodney Bayham an African American. Make Edward a misogynist and Yvonne a virgin bride with no contextual alteration; make Lily Briscoe a musician or Stephen Daedalus an altar boy abused by a priest, with no stylistic shift.

28. Describe Rinaldi's death (a) via tertiary syphilis, (b) in battle, (c) as a suicide. In each of the six authorial voices.

29. Translate twenty lines in any of the books into any language available to you, then translate it back (without consulting the original). Compare.

30. Enlarge and alter a sentence, a paragraph, a page in each of the six instances; make the sentence a paragraph, paragraph a page, and page a brief chapter with no additional information or extraneous voice.

31. Create thirty additional exercises such as the above.

32. Create your own short story in which characters such as M. Laruelle or Mr. Ramsay appear, though parenthetically; then do the same employing them as the tale's protagonists.

33. Describe some recognizable locale (the Diag, the Arboretum, the corner of Fifty-Seventh Street and Fifth Avenue, Disneyland, etc.) in the terms of Hemingway, Ford, Woolf, et al. Do this as if your protagonist is seeing this scene for the first time, then last.

34. Discover and defend new titles for each of the books (e.g., *A Separate Peace, The Saddest Story*); create epigraphs for each.

35. Create a masque, ballet, screenplay, or mime in which a characteristic gesture of a protagonist in each of the six instances is otherwise displayed.

36. Inanimate objects: the rowboat in *A Farewell to Arms,* the coffin and stable in *As I Lay Dying,* etc. Ruminate about them in the authorial voice, then that of one or more of the ancillary characters.

37. Introduce the (biographical) personalities of Hemingway, Lowry, Woolf et al. in a scene deploying their principal creations; have Geoffrey confront Malcolm, Darl meet Bill, Stephen meet James Joyce, etc.

38. Provide the birth, marriage, and death announcements of Lily Briscoe, Stephen Daedalus, and Addie Bundren; write a dream sequence for each.

39. Compose an epistolary exchange between Florence Hurlbird and Jimmy, a series of songs by Geoffrey Firmin about Yvonne, such that the reader's sense of their relationships will be entirely changed.

40. Revise any three of these exercises, once completed, back into your own voice.

41. Having reread a page in any of these books (but without a conscious attempt at memorization), attempt to reproduce it.

42. Write a collective novel, with two or more collaborators from the class, having agreed in advance as to the broad outlines of plot, characterization, and so forth—without continual cross-checking. So that you are solely responsible for Chapters 1, 4, 7, 10 and ignorant of 2, 3, 5, 6, etc. Do so in the several styles.

43. Combine exercises 4 and 9 above but in terms of imitation, not parody. Have Joyce write of water as if he were Hemingway, not aping him; have Ford attempt to reproduce—for instance as in 40—the Cora chapters from Faulkner; have Lowry replicate Woolf.

44. Recreate act 4 of *Hamlet* in at least three of the six voices.

45. Find passages of twenty lines or longer in each of the six books that do not signal signature. Reproduce them without identification (altering only the tell-tale details) and try to fool your friends.

46. Create forty-five additional exercises such as the above, but with different texts.

47. Take Faulkner's Nobel Prize acceptance speech and have it delivered by Hemingway, Ford, Woolf, Joyce, and/or Lowry instead. What changes, what stays the same?

48. Rewrite the first chapter of the books here under discussion via a prologue that reverses our understanding of what is to follow, so that the tale will be materially altered—Jewel doesn't leave but settles down to the Bundren farm; a memoir written by the surviving son of Frederick and Catherine; etc.

49. From internal evidence only, and without consulting the author's next work (or ignoring what you a priori know), invent the first chapter of the six subsequent novels. Do this consciously as sequel, but in stylistic not substantive terms; we're not talking here about *Son of the Good Soldier* or *The Ramsays Return to the Lighthouse*.

50. Write *Son of the Good Soldier* and *The Ramsays Return to the Lighthouse*.

Remarks: It should be obvious that the above are signposts, largely, and not the road itself. Also, that anyone who could manage all fifty of these exercises within a fourteen-week span would be so preternaturally gifted as to have no use or need for any of these exercises. Or, indeed, this course. (Though it's worth remarking that the gift of imitation is a discrete skill sometimes; the first-rate forger might prove wholly unoriginal.) Further, and as a couple of the exercises suggest, there should be nothing sacrosanct about the propositions here—one could as easily invent a wholly separate list. Or combine or reverse or ignore them. What I've tried to do, in effect, is indicate a way of thinking about prose in general—a way that combines a craftsman-like appreciation of the manner in which books are put together with a glad willingness to take them apart. Though I think numbers 24 and 26 might well result in an improved page of Lowry or Ford, it's certainly not the point of this course that we should meddle endlessly with what's left well enough alone. That would be idiot's delight, even if by term's end we were *idiots savants*.

Rather, the aim of these exercises is twofold. First, and clearly, it's one way to learn to read several twentieth-century masterpieces (the bulk of which, not incidentally, I assume you've read before. Which is one of the reasons I picked them; rereading provides a different approach to a text.) But the second aim is a little less clear and bears explaining. It has something to do with the nature of language and our presumed literacy—a natal familiarity with English that, more often than not in the contemporary writer, breeds contempt. No one presumes to give a dance recital without having first mastered the rudiments of dance, to perform Mozart before they've learned scales, or to enter a weight-lifting contest if they've never hoisted weights. Yet because we've been reading since five, we blithely assume we can read; because we scrawled our signature when six, we glibly aspire to write.

Anyone who does even a few of these exercises will have to revise such assumptions. Our language is a rich and complex thing, and the conscious, conscientious study of rhetoric has largely disappeared. There are books on the subject, of course, and now and again the academy asseverates that style's a thing to keep. But if you cannot tell an oxymoron from chiasmus by term's end you will nonetheless have learned something about the freedom within limits that is the root and force of syntax. Do as many of these exercises as you can plausibly manage, then scrap them and begin.

As stated earlier, I taught this course often and often. The writers and the novels vary; methodology, however, stayed the same. This particular syllabus describes a course I offered in 1995, and here are five examples of student response to these exercises. They deal, turn by turn, with the styles of William Faulkner, Virginia Woolf, Ford Madox Ford, Ernest Hemingway, and James Joyce. Each of these extracts strikes me as first-rate, and each signaled— at least to their teacher—the promise of a career to come. It has been a promise fulfilled.

The first of these authors (arranged alphabetically) was still an undergraduate when he composed the following paragraphs; the other four were enrolled in the MFA Program at the University of Michigan, now known as the Helen Zell Writers' Program. At the end of the semester, we produced a pamphlet representing work achieved as an "Anthology of Imitations." I'm grateful, in each instance, for permission to (re)print.

Dean Bakopolous: The writer imagines Quentin's suicide note from another of Faulkner's great experimental works, *The Sound and the Fury*. This is a false document but written in the full tide of Faulknerian—or, perhaps, Compsonian—rhetoric. Mr. Bakopolous is the author of three novels: *Please Don't Come Back from the Moon, My American Unhappiness,* and *Summerlong.* He has received a Guggenheim Fellowship, two NEA Fellowships, and is writer-in-residence at Grinnell College.

Father, you said this was the reductio ad absurdum of all human experience, this time and I cant outrun time anymore. Now I am writing this and I have my back turned from the sash so I cant see the shadows and then I cant know what the time is you said Christ wasn't crucified but that he was worn away by the minute clicking of gears and then father I am no Christ but I too have worn away or am worn away. Some don't understand this and then I say they never had a sister did they? Of course not Father and I didn't commit incest but Caddy is still unvirgin just like you had said and then you sent out Mr. and Mrs. Jason Compson III to announce the marriage of and so you were right worn away by little wheels and then there is nothing and you were right the reductio ad absurdum of human experience.

You will find my things in order. I folded them and gave away what should be given away and the rest will be sent to you. Sell it if you think anyone would buy it like they bought Benjy's pasture so I could go to Harvard and now changing his name didnt change anyone's luck but he will not know how stupid and useless and ridiculous he looks at watches and clocks and sees nothing a sphere with hands pointing at numbers everything ticking and moving and it means nothing. Benjy the son of mine old age Mother said and if I could hear mother call me son and then Id say mother mother mother.

Caddy I cannot forget and I drew my fists Dalton Ames and Caddy cannot be watched anymore and watch Caddy for us all and keep her and I know you don't care that she is unvirgin but Father I think of that and cannot sleep at night and see the shadows move across the wall with the moonlight coming in and I don't even look at the clock but I can hear it in Shreve's room and I know all that wearing down and Jesus Christ wearing down like me like you said I could forget and no I no I cannot forget it. Fui. Non fui. I am I was. This is the saddest of all and there is nothing else I want and I remember the despair and its not even real without time and so I am doing it and I feel almost good that I am going to do it because it is something not like the nothing I did when Dalton Ames and tell Caddy I did it but not because of anything she did but because of time and like you said it wears us down and you can forget it if you want but I cant anyway. I am I was. Non fui. Fui. The reductio ad absurdum of all human experience.

Michael Byers: Here the writer also imagines a scene from William Faulkner's *The Sound and the Fury,* this time as if composed by Virginia Woolf. Looking for his niece, Jason Compson has an argument with a man with a hatchet—an unlikely encounter in Woolf's fictive world. Mr. Byers is the author of the short story collection *The Coast of Good Intentions,* and the novels *Long for This World* and *Percival's Planet.* His work has received recognition from the Henfield Foundation, the American Academy of Arts and Letters, and the Whiting Foundation. He has taught in the MFA Program at the University of Michigan, Ann Arbor, since 2006.

He stepped forward and swung the hatchet, and Jason stepped backward, fearing at once that he had come to the wrong place; that he had mistaken this town for another; that in his reverie over the wheel on the dusty road he had driven too far, was now in another state, another country, where a different language was spoken, and as a man will hesitate on the edge of an uncertain opinion before speaking—judging those around him, whether they might refute him, or know better than he, and so shame him with a sideways glance, or snicker and draw in the dirt with their toes, being men who knew the cotton trade—Jason hung for a moment suspended, before he began falling backward.

He lay still on the floor. Perhaps, Jason felt, one helped oneself out of such trouble slowly by laying hold of some little odd or end, some sound, some sight, which might attach itself to something else, and something else again, leading him back, at last, to the world. He looked; but his sight was blurred: yellow shapes rolled here and there on the floor in front of him; there was only the sound of the man's footsteps and his high peculiar song. He sat up; he held his white hat in his hands. He saw the man again, still approaching. With some amusement, for when one is stunned, one's moods are unpredictable, he looked at the man, his hunched back, the raised hatchet, this man who was so much himself, and yet so far from himself (later he would imagine this man coming across the porch at him in the evenings, as if he had followed him home, stomping the floor), but beyond that he thought, watching him with eagerness, tipping his body back, that he wished some part of himself to be removed, that part which took him here in the dust to find a niece he did not love, and it was as if the hatchet were running its blade over him, gently, to find that piece of him he did not wish to have any longer, and when it was gone he would be flooded with an intense delight.

Paisley Rekdal: The writer here takes the protagonist of Ford Madox Ford's *The Good Soldier*—whose opening line is "This is the saddest story I have ever heard"—and renders it in the terms of

Greek tragedy, deploying the story of Oedipus Rex in a quasi-comic vein. Ms. Rekdal is the author of the non-fiction *The Night My Mother Met Bruce Lee*, and such books of poetry as *A Crash of Rhinos, Six Girls without Pants, Animal Eye, Imaginary Vessels,* and most recently, *Nightingale*. She has received, among other awards, the Guggenheim Fellowship and an NEA Fellowship. She teaches at the University of Utah and is poet laureate of the State of Utah.

This is the second saddest story I have ever heard. I knew my wife as well as it is possible to know anybody—perhaps too well on certain occasions—and yet in a sense, I knew nothing about her. At first I took this to mean that I didn't understand people from Thebes—that part of the country from which my wife came—but now I'm not sure that I know anything about the matter at all. I don't mean to say that I've never been to Thebes or met people from Thebes, only that I have never sounded out the depths of a Theban heart. Perhaps I've sounded out the shallows or even the shores a little, but certainly not the depths. Of course I was acquainted with people from my Thebes, living, as I did, only a slight distance from it with my parents in Eleusis, a town famous for its ophthalmologists and where I now presently reside with a servant. You will gather from this statement that one of us has, as the saying is, "eye problems," and from the statement that my servant is a transcriber, that I am the sufferer.

For nine years we lived together in a perfect intimacy. It was like stepping the exact pattern of a chorus. You can't kill a chorus de Coeur. We were like two dithyrambs of the soul, Jocasta and I. Sometimes I recount how my married hours were spent, and think I couldn't have been apart from her more than a few minutes total in our nine years together. What with her heart and her medicines and her fears of letting me out of her sight too long, I was always underfoot. As husband and wife I suppose we were more closely knit than most family members could ever hope to be. Perverse! Disgusting! But true.

I mention these things now because I wonder if there is anything to guide us. Are we to act on impulse alone? Perhaps impulse does not exist. Perhaps the only intangible guide available to us is our own innate sense of truth, of prophecy, of inherent human limitation. Indeed, what at first seems to be simple circumstance or impulse might, in fact, reveal itself to be a decision of the most conscious kind—to wound others, to wound ourselves because it is that in which we take most pleasure. But I'm no longer sure. It is all a darkness to me . . .

I thought I knew the worst of her at the end of that trial. I knew for sure I had killed Laius, and that Timon's depiction of her had been true: she had loved him desperately enough to take his murderous doppelganger for a husband. But I hadn't known the rest. Timon had to tell me. "You see," he began, "there was a child from her first marriage."

Jess Row: The writer here transposes a scene (chapter 20) in *A Farewell to Arms* from Europe in the First World War to Hong Kong in the winter of 1997–1998, during the heart of the Asian financial meltdown. Mr. Row has published two collections of short stories, *The Train to Lo Wu* and *Nobody Ever Gets Lost,* as well as the novel *Your Face in Mine.* His 2019 work of non-fiction is titled *White Flights: Race, Fiction, and the American Imagination.* He is the recipient of, among other honors, a Guggenheim Fellowship and the Whiting Award.

One Sunday in the afternoon we went to the races. Bridget went too and Arthur Ko, the boy who had been in Peregrine Fixed Assets when the scandal fell and the company folded the same day. The girls put on their makeup after lunch while Ko and I stood on the balcony and read the past performances of the horses and the predictions in the paper. Ko checked his pager every five minutes and he did not care much about these races but read the racing paper constantly and kept track of all the horses for something to do. He said the horses were a terrible lot but they were the best we could do with the Invitational in two weeks. The owners were saving the good horses for the Invitational.

Ah-Leung liked him and gave him tips. Leung won on nearly every race but disliked to give tips because it brought down the prices. The racing was very crooked. Though the Jockey Club put up a good front only the clubhouse members heard the good tips and their runners who could be bribed but for a small fortune in American dollars. Leung's information was good but I hated to ask him because sometimes he did not answer, and always you could see it hurt him to tell you, but he felt obligated to tell us for some reason and he hated less to tell Ko. Ko's family had been hurt badly by the loss of income, a building deal in Toronto had broken up, and Leung had also suffered terrible losses in the market collapse and so he liked Ko. Leung never told his wife what horses he was playing and she won or lost, mostly lost, and talked on her mobile all the time.

We four drove through the tunnel to Happy Valley in Ko's Jaguar convertible. It was a lovely day and we drove along the green hillsides and the Repulse Bay beaches and along the jetties east of Aberdeen and into the tunnel past the sign that listed the number of accidents for the year. There were villas with stucco walls and lines of palms and banana and cypress and the water sparkling and the humps of the outlying islands across the channel. We could look across the water and see junks and sailboats on the sparkling waves and the mountains of Lantau to the north. There were many cars parking in the member's lot and the men at the Gate let us in without cards because Ko leaned over and said something quick and hard in Cantonese about Ah-Leung. We left the car, bought racing cards, and took the elevator to the clubhouse floor. The carpet there was thick and deep and the windows were polished so that we might have been outside, but the members talked quietly and the waiters made no sound when they walked. We went out onto the viewing balcony and saw people that we knew and leaned over the rail and borrowed binoculars to watch the horses.

Leah Stewart: Here the writer imagines Hamlet's mother, Queen Gertrude, as Joyce's Molly Bloom in her soliloquy. In Shakespeare's phrase she "post(s) with such dexterity to incestuous sheets"; this parody gives those sheets a twist. Ms. Stewart has published several novels, among them *Body of a Girl, The Myth of You and Me, Husband and Wife,* and *The New Neighbors.* Her most recent title is *What You Don't Know about Charlie Outlaw,* and she directs the writing program at the University of Cincinnati, Ohio.

> Yes, here he is again his great fat belly up against my back he's never come to bed this soon since that time after little Margaret took up with that young officer after he thought he had a hold of her and she gone before sunrise and that lieutenant too the one with the dark hair telling me he wanted to be of any service and to the king too of course still hes not jealous of the young ones yes hes been somewhere this afternoon or Im sure he wouldnt have been here lumped up behind me before 2 I wonder who it is this time I only hope he keeps it quiet not that cook she makes a lovely stew all carroty and potatoes and onions Id like to see him do without a good cook I suppose he'd have me down in the kitchen next rousting up whatever he took a fancy for never one to ignore his appetites even in the middle of a play he'd stop and call for a plate of something when was it he had that craving for a mutton leg left the lord of somewhere or other waiting while he sent down to the kitchen for it O its surprising he can even get up on those young girls anymore youd think hed need a stepstool the night Claudius ran his hand up the side of my leg underneath the banquet table I

opened my legs such a feeling it gave me his hand was gone O he
was careful then lifting his glass to me though I let on I didn't know
what it meant when I lifted my glass I always liked red wine he used
to pour it on my belly the King and lick it off it stained the linens
he used to say hed hang the sheet out after as though Id been a
virgin 20 times over bleeding and bleeding you never know how
theyll take it he used to want it more than rubbing blood on my
belly with it wanting me to say something smutty O hurts like the
first time wanting me to be the servant girl and he the king taking
me up against the wall in some back corner Lord God Ive thought
of it myself putting my hair in plaits Ive a body like a school girl still
though in the light the lines on my belly show surprising one of the
servants in the wine cellar where its dark O that one with the small
round bottom and the dark eyes pretty as a woman's I suppose the
floor would be cold Id look up and see all bottles of red wine Id
better sleep soon how can I with his great heavy leg across my belly
he used to be all lines like that statue in the hall that Hamlet
brought me lines underneath his skin and I could feel a straining in
his back when he was on me O wasn't I the born fool not to know
hed get all doughy that great belly of his pressed against my belly
and I thinking only of the sound it makes a suck-suck sticking to
my skin and pulling off when he moves . . .

Hamlet always creeping about the castle reading though I never
see him turn a page he says he is reading and what else would he be
doing always holding a book though some appear to be learned
when they aren't like that what was his name Reynaldo no thats that
servant of Polonius pretending to my father he was educated when I
declare to God he couldn't read a word or even write his own name
I often feel I want to kiss him not dirty or anything just like a
mother on that lovely young mouth theres real poetry for you a
different kind of feeling they talk about love but they want you to
lift your skirts Ill let him know whats good for the goose or I mean
the gander Ill lift my skirts up in the tower as well him as another I
thought that time I first saw him and he asked though my father

had sent me for yes and then he asked me would I say yes my queen and I a girl of 13 I put my arms around him and I said yes I will Yes.

The elegant stylist John Cheever once told me that, when he gave his students writing exercises, he felt honor-bound to produce his own versions as well. As a sixth entry into the imitation sweepstakes—and because there were six authors in the syllabus—I therefore offer up my own attempt at exercise 47. This is William Faulkner's Nobel Prize acceptance speech, delivered in Stockholm in 1950, as if pronounced by Malcolm Lowry in a bar. Lowry was a polyglot and an alcoholic; so too is his character, Geoffrey Firmin—who here mourns the absence of his estranged wife, Yvonne.

I feel this glass of mezcal was set before me neither with maleficent intention nor commercial inattention but in order to create out of the materials of agave and the human spirit something absent heretofore. So this libation is only mine in trust. It will not be difficult (*Pulque!*) to find a dedication for the liquid part of it commensurate with the purpose and significance of its origin: *Oaxaca, you city of sorrows!* But I would like to do the same with the pickled egg as well, by using this moment as a pinnacle from which I might be listened to by the young men and women already dedicated to the same anguish and travail, the same creative aspiration, among whom stands already that one who will someday order what I am ordering now: *Mezcal! Ancor un Baccio! Une larme!* Edging up against the same match-charred and ash-encrusted time-stained counter, that acolyte will stand before the microphone upon this raised and august dais as does your tide-tongued speaker (*Hola, Hombre!*), attempting to make sense of the trajectory by which we hurtle headlong into the gaping ravine, the barranca, Hell's bunker. (*Que tal?*) It is the Samaritan's privilege—indeed, his obligation, *Slainte, Santé, Cheers, Prosit, Proust!*—to help man endure by lifting his heart as well as his replenished glass, and in so doing remind us of the courage and honor and hope and pride and compassion and pity and sacrifice which have been the glory of the past.

Our tragedy today is a general and universal physical fear so long sustained by now that we can even bear it. We write not of love but of lust, of defeats in which nobody loses anything of value, of victories without hope and, worst of all, without pity or compassion. There are no longer problems of the spirit. *Le Gusta esta Mezcal? Que es Suyo?* There are only problems of the glands. For ah, Yvonne, these shreds and remnants of the scarf you wore, this scrap of silk with its design of butterflies reminds me of—as if I needed reminding, as if I could ever forget!—the soft tingle of your neck and clavicle and arm on or more properly adjacent to mine: *jingle, jingle, little surcingle,* reminding me as well of sundered volcanoes (the severance! the parting!), the *huracan* testifying so suggestively to intercourse on either side of what was once Atlantis: *come back to me, if only for a day!* It is easy enough to say that man is immortal simply because he will endure: that when the last dingdong of doom has clanged and faded from the last worthless rock hanging tideless in the last red and dying evening, that even then there will still be one more sound: that of his puny inexhaustible voice, still talking. *Bibendum Bibendoom, Boom.* I refuse to accept this. I believe that man will not merely endure: he will by repetition and incantation and imitation prevail. *No se puede vivir sin amar.* For, ah, how alike are the cries of love to those of the dying, the cries of the dying to those of love. The heart, the glands, the endocrines and end of man, the endless recurrence recurring. And now there is only the question: When will this glass be filled? " 'Mezcal,' the Consul said."

One additional entry. At the University of Michigan, in 2004, a student enrolled in the MFA program for which I served as director. She came from the deep South and was ill at ease. Arriving, she told me in private, she felt homesick for Mississippi and her family in DeLisle. Further, the young woman suffered from migraines and was horrified by snow. She seemed hesitant to speak in class, unhappy and alone. Her debut was inauspicious, her first set of exercises argued—or so I feared—a tin ear. I worried she'd not stay the course, either literally or metaphorically, and told her to take all the time she required in order to write the assignments and not to join the discussions until she had something to say.

This went on for some time. Her imitations of Hemingway, Ford, and Woolf were, to put it bluntly, second-rate. The echoes were muffled, the rhetoric inexact. But then we came to William Faulkner, and the student *got* it; it was almost as though Faulkner too attended class and she were channeling him. Her language had been static; it now grew electric, and everyone in the seminar room shared my opinion and praise. The landscape, the descriptive prose, the dialogue, the characters all echoed the great original, but in an original mode. From that moment on the student was a full and eager member of our group; her talent fairly blazed. In all my years of teaching I have not, before or since, seen such a transformation; by borrowing the syntax and inflections of a dead southern master, the writer found her voice.

That voice belongs to Jesmyn Ward. Her first novel, *Where the Line Bleeds* (2008), begins with a passage she produced for "Strategies in Prose," and by now Ms. Ward's own language has been much copied and honored. She has received the MacArthur

("Genius") Award and the Mildred and Harold Strauss Livings Award from the American Academy. Her 2011 novel, *Salvage the Bones,* won the National Book Award for Fiction. Her memoir, *Men We Reaped* (2013), about the deaths of her brother and four other young men, demonstrates full authorial assurance. In *The Fire This Time* (2016), she contributed an essay to and edited a collection of tributes to James Baldwin, referencing his classic *The Fire Next Time* (1963). Her most recent novel, *Sing, Unburied, Sing* (2017), was published to widespread acclaim and, for the second time—the only time such an honor has been twice accorded to a woman—won the National Book Award in Fiction. Though there are echoes, still, of Faulkner, hers has become a style absorbed and voiced in a new key. If only in this one career—but there are many, many more—I feel the value of close study of the work of other authors has been amply shown.

6 originality

Time now to write of that rare
thing, originality—the opposite
of imitation and its outlier,
plagiarism. It's the pearl among
white peas. As Aristotle, that great
classifier, taught us: we see the
difference only in those things
that are in essence similar. One
might compare a shoe and boot,
but not a shoe and boat. One
might compare a horse and cow,
but not a horse and house. (Unless
the category is orthography, of
which more in a minute . . .) They
are by nature different entities,
and to draw comparisons or assert
equivalence is to overreach.

The Metaphysical Poets,
however, made a point of just
such excess—comparing, say, two
separated lovers to a compass-set,

as in John Donne's "A Valediction Forbidding Mourning" (1611–1612). Here are the poem's three closing stanzas:

> If they be two, they are two so
>   As stiff twin compasses are two;
> Thy soul, the fixed foot, makes no show
>   To move, but doth, if the other do.
>
> And though it in the center sit,
>   Yet when the other far doth roam,
> It leans and hearkens after it,
>   And grows erect, as that comes home.
>
> Such wilt thou be to me, who must,
>   Like th' other foot, obliquely run;
> Thy firmness makes my circle just,
>   And makes me end where I begun.

By the time the simile has been elaborated on, and the comparison established, the metaphysical "conceit" comes clear. Donne's daring (and sexually charged) assertion that the "fixed foot . . . grows erect" makes a kind of sense at poem's end that felt strained at the beginning, almost as though he wins an argument with his protesting wife about the need for travel. It's a tour de force of verbal wit and takes some getting used to, but the very implausibility of the comparison renders it indelible. Another enduring phrase in "A Valediction"—"like gold to airy thinness beat"—does much the same, and what this sort of poem manages is a categorical shift, so that compass and lovers are one. The "horse and house," the "boot and boat," have fused.

In terms of spelling, however, one could readily compare—by shifting just one letter—these two improbable pairings: horse and house, boat and boot. (Again, let me remember the clumsy boy in high school making inadvertent puns while setting moveable type.) There are errata in printing and errors of orthography or grammar in almost every text. For now that we have books (and iPads and computer screens), the acquisition of language has shifted from the phonographic to the photographic; we *see* what once we *heard*. The photographic memory is a rare but not vanishingly rare gift in our species; the phonographic memory has been almost entirely lost. Much follows from that change.

One kind of change is site-specific (sight-specific?). Because words can be transmitted in silence, there's less need for physical performance and recollected speech. We no longer listen but look. Since time out of mind, young writers have studied at the feet of predecessors, yet once a book exists in print it makes no actual difference if they share a room. The apprentice need not have a drink with Christopher Marlowe or travel with Charles Baudelaire or take tea with Emily Brontë in order to profit from their example and learn a few tricks of their trade. The mastermaker may be dead or distant; the work—with luck—lives on.

Yet more and more these years, and particularly in America, we've come to believe that proximity counts, and that this craft, which must be learned, can in fact be taught. It's a limited task, perhaps; the best writing teacher in the history of the business has never made a silk purse of a sow's ear with no talent. And—though this is harder to prove, since evidence is necessarily absent—the worst of writing teachers has never destroyed a true gift. So what we at most are able to do is offer up assistance, reducing the period of trial-and-error apprenticeship by advising the aspirant author how to solve certain problems of craft. What else do such programs provide; why else do we enroll and what does the degree of master of fine arts confer? A community, yes, a sense of shared endeavor, yes, but the young writer by and large is after self-expression. Therefore what we as teachers offer is the time and space—the necessary space and time—for both worker and work to mature.

It doesn't happen overnight and doesn't happen easily. It's an individuated process and one that requires patience. But unlike a lot of other skills—the skills of a basketball player, say, or a ballerina—the odds improve over time. It's the rare athlete or performer who's better at fifty than twenty; some say this holds equally true for prodigies in mathematics and chess. Certain painters and musicians *do* do their best work early, but only the exceptional author does her or his own best work first. I mean "exceptional" here as in the "exception to the rule"; the general truth is—since our raw material is the stuff of earned experience—that talent enlarges with age. I'm not suggesting the centenarian is necessarily more accomplished than the nonagenarian, the nonagenarian than the octogenarian, and so on down the line. That's obviously wrong. But it does seem as though most young writers know the best work lies ahead. How sad, in fact, to believe the reverse, to tell yourself the best work lies behind you, and there's nothing left but diminution and decline . . .

James Joyce was an excellent student. His *A Portrait of the Artist as a Young Man* describes young Stephen Dedalus as a questing and questioning intelligence. When, in the famous final phrase, Joyce's alter ego goes "in the smithy of my soul to forge the uncreated conscience of my race," he takes on a project of overweening ambition. The "silence, exile, and cunning" that are Stephen's stated tools with which to "forge" that conscience were Joyce's weapons also; he seeks both that which can be revealed and what remains unknowable. The work of a forger is to fuse hot metal, as might a laboring smithy at the blacksmith's forge; it's also to falsify a document and profit from the lie. Reading the writer's completed works—*Dubliners, Portrait of the Artist, Ulysses,* and *Finnegans Wake*—is to chart a course of almost constant innovation and stylistic shifts. (This holds true for the poetry also, and the work in progress not ushered into print.) Scarcely any other major author was so various in his rhetoric or changeable from book to book. Each time he started out he started out afresh.

The equivalent in the visual arts is, perhaps, Picasso. No viewer of the early work—or even of the Rose and Blue periods—could have predicted Cubism or Guernica; no reader of *Dubliners* would have guessed at the language of *Finnegans Wake.* There's a through-line in the author's ear—his usage of the aural faculty in dialogue and puns—and it grows more definite as the eyesight fades. By the end of his life Joyce was clinically blind, and the sound of things gained nearly total primacy. The final volume makes more sense when read aloud. But always Joyce was willing—anxious, even—to cross borders; his art had been transgressive from the first.

Take the figure of Leopold Bloom. To have equated Odysseus, the noble Greek, with a Jewish salesman is to defy those categories and classifications adduced above. To equate the town of Dublin in the early twentieth century with ancient Attica is to do the same. To have the faithless Molly stand in for faithful Penelope, to have our hero sit on the toilet and eat pigs' knuckles and, watching a lame girl, masturbate, is to violate tenets of fictive decorum and engender a new mode of prose. In one sense, the metaphysical conceit embraced by Donne and Marvell is revived at book length in *Ulysses,* but the analogies and parallels all have been disguised; it took years before the *ur*-text would emerge. (Let me repeat, at the risk of repetition, that this is a prime example of use of the "backstory" referred to earlier; Michael Cunningham and Zadie Smith et al. make their indebtedness clear. But until the "trot" published by Stuart Gilbert in 1930, few readers recognized the template of the *Odyssey;* it had been well hidden.) Originality claims Joyce as one of its great avatars: a rule-breaker establishing rules.

I write this from the island, on the Hermes 3000 he left. I suppose it was provided for that purpose—it's nearly new, and Blumenberg himself preferred charcoal or India ink. The ribbon is black. It has elite type. It has a pleasing gray-green tint, and only after three days did I recognize the case as plastic, not metal. There's an instruction sheet. This is the first such portable I've used, and the small precise shapes of the letters seem almost as if they were print. I take some comfort in that. He must have wanted me to feel at home—he amassed all the needful supplies. He'd hoped I might remain, it seems, or could not keep his promise that the Coast Guard would arrive.

Of late I've learned to make deductions, learned to speculate. Blumenberg would say that even such language betrays me—that "speculate" and "deduction" are words to use for business, not art. "You're an accountant," he'd say. "Stop toting up accounts."

These are the first two paragraphs of a novel I wrote and abandoned forty years ago. It was called *Blumenberg the Elder* and conceived of as a first-person comic novel whose *donnée* encompassed the art world and the course of a career. My protagonist was to have been an aging sculptor who staged his own death falsely in order to withdraw from the public arena and, by no means incidentally, to increase the market value of his work. My narrator was a gullible young man who served as Blumenberg's assistant and fell in love with the sculptor's secretary and found himself abandoned by her too. The locale was an imagined island off the coast of Massachusetts—near Martha's Vineyard and Naushon and Cuttyhunk—where the artist's body (or a simulacrum thereof) washed up.

Looking back on *Blumenberg the Elder,* I'm struck by its old-fashioned feel, the way my narrator must use what's now a relic—a typewriter named after a Greek messenger-god, with ribbons and a tape recorder—to unspool his tale. Some of this was inadvertent; those were the tools I used. The Hermes 3000 was my own chosen instrument those years, and Eaton's Corrasable twenty-weight bond the paper I preferred. The novel did have promise and its premise was not unoriginal: it was intended as a narrative romp, and I composed it with élan. Indeed, I've never written anything with such self-delighting pleasure or so rapidly; I drafted the four-hundred-page adventure in three months.

But it was foredoomed from the start. I see now what I failed to see then: the book was inauthentic from first to final line. I was borrowing from *Henderson the Rain King* by Saul Bellow, from the prose of John Barth and Stanley Elkin and other authors who wrote in the first person with *brio*. A novella by John Fowles, *The Ebony Tower,* served as a model too. My own effort at the comic or ironic mode was far less accomplished than the work of the practitioners I hoped to emulate. The voice proved an uneasy blend of rhetorical extravagance and aw-shucks down-home chit-chat; I was trying on their attitudes and dialogue patterns for size.

Nor did the first person suit me, since my narrator, Kenneth Potter, moved back and forth between all-knowing and sublimely ignorant; the revelations which were meant to take a reader by surprise took Kenneth by surprise as well, and much of what he learned or claimed to know was fake. His slow-dawning awareness of how he'd been "played" by the sculptor was a plot device only, and hollow; the rabbit I pulled from the hat at book's end had shown its white ears all along.

Most importantly, perhaps, I never quite decided if the title character was an original artist or a fraud. He moved with dizzying alacrity from shaman to showman, from craftsman to lout. And since a central theme of the novel had to do with value as opposed to valuation, this attempt to "have it both ways" was bound to fail. Blumenberg was either a genius or charlatan; he could not be both.

Many authors have a flat-out failure in their history, a work they shelved or burned or left unfinished. This was mine. In the decades since my editor and agent and the one or two close readers to whom I showed the text looked at me with kind concern and collective dismissiveness, I have not cracked the pages of the book. But looking at it now again I see—in the terms of imitation and originality that have organized this discussion—how much I deployed the former, how little I had of the latter. I've heard writers say of their novels, "This is the book I was born to write," but *Blumenberg the Elder* lay stillborn on the page. I include it in this chapter because it demonstrates (to this author's satisfaction, at least) a young man's search for voice, and how he'd yet to locate tone or key. There was next to nothing authentic in concept or execution; I had published several books by then, but was an apprentice or at best a journeyman laborer still . . .

Let's look again at the first paragraph of *Blumenberg the Elder*. I want to ring some changes on it; in the hope of earned improvement, I want to attempt to revise. To start with, let's erase the first person and tell this from the third-person point of view.

> He writes this from the island, on the Hermes 3000 he left. He supposes it has been provided for that purpose—it's nearly new, and Blumenberg himself preferred charcoal or India ink. The ribbon is black. It has elite type. It has a pleasing gray-green tint, and only after three days did he recognize the case as plastic, not metal. There's an instruction sheet. This is the first such portable he's used, and the small precise shapes of the letters seem almost as if they were print. He takes some comfort in that. He must have wanted him to feel at home—he amassed all the needful supplies. He'd hoped he might remain, it seems, or could not keep his promise that the Coast Guard would arrive.

There are obvious problems here. The doubling usage of "he" feels clumsy and fails to make a distinction between the "he" that (in the first-person narrative version) is the speaker and the "he" of Blumenberg. The lack of clarity confuses, and it must be fixed. This entails more than the mere word-change from "I" to "he," and requires some small revision. As in:

> He writes this from the island, on the Hermes 3000 that Blumenberg left. He supposes it has been provided for that purpose—it's nearly new, and the artist himself preferred to use charcoal or India ink. The ribbon is black. It has elite type. It has a pleasing gray-green tint, and only after three days does he recognize the case is plastic, not metal. There's an instruction sheet. This is the first such portable Kenneth Potter used, and the small precise shapes of the letters seem almost as if they are print. He takes some comfort in that. Blumenberg must have wanted him to feel at home—he amassed all the needful supplies. The sculptor hoped he might remain, it seems, or could not keep his promise that the Coast Guard would arrive.

This is marginally better, but it still seems confusing. I should probably have identified the young man early on, as in "only after three days does Kenneth Potter recognize the case . . ." Or even "Kenneth Potter writes this from the island . . ." This would have had the advantage of establishing the opposition or *agon* of the two central characters, so that we might recognize from novel's start there are a pair of players with dissimilar names; one has only a surname, most likely Jewish, the other's decisively WASP. One other addition, in the first sentence, is the word "that" after "Hermes 3000." For reasons of clarity and rhythm it seemed to me needful to separate the name of the typewriter from the name of the man who abandoned it: "Hermes 3000 Blumenberg left" might sow some small confusion.

Further, there's a question about the appropriate usage of "it seems" in the last sentence of the paragraph. Since the narrative vantage is now the third person, the question arises as to "seeming." Wouldn't the author be sure? Kenneth Potter might have been confused; the narrator would not. Too, the word "seems" had been used before ("seem almost as if they are print") and though this book will be importantly about reality, appearance, and the distinction between them, one doesn't want to show one's hand too soon.

Now let's change the tense as well as point of view, and render this all in the past. Though present-tense usage has become, of late, routine, it remains the case that third-person past tense is the time-honored mode of prose fiction. And if we elect the omniscient authorial voice—still the gold standard for the novel—the problematic nature of "it seems" is no longer a problem; the narrator knows what the character can't. The novel's opening beat would therefore read:

Kenneth Potter wrote this from the island, on the Hermes 3000 that Blumenberg left. He supposed it was provided for that purpose—it was nearly new, and Blumenberg himself preferred charcoal or India ink. The ribbon was black. It had elite type. The Hermes had a pleasing gray-green tint, and only after three days did Potter recognize the case as plastic, not metal. There was an instruction sheet. This was the first such portable he'd used, and the small precise shapes of the letters seemed almost as if they were print. He took some comfort in that. Blumenberg must have wanted him to feel at home—he'd amassed all the needful supplies. The sculptor hoped he might remain, it seemed, or could not keep his promise that the Coast Guard would arrive.

Here the pluperfect was needful. But a couple of minor altera-
tions follow. I find the sentence "There was an instruction sheet"
an irrelevance and think it should be cut. And I'd change the
"seemed" to "looked," so that the sequence reads: "the case was
plastic, not metal. This was the first such portable he'd used, and
the small precise shapes of the letters looked almost like print."
Too, and though I welcome and would try to keep the detail that
the Hermes 3000 deploys an elite type face, the line "It had elite
type" now seems a non sequitur. The indefinite article "it" belongs to the ribbon, not typewriter, and because of its placement
misleads. Further (and since the book deals with the visual arts) I
like the juxtaposition of "The ribbon was black" to "The Hermes
had a pleasing gray-green tint"; their coloration counts. So it
makes sense, or would have, to move the sentence; Potter is/was
an elitist, and he'd of course prefer a typeface with that name. Yet
"the sculptor hoped he might remain" is still a touch confusing,
and could be improved by substituting a descriptive for the pronoun. At length we have:

> Kenneth Potter wrote from the island, on the Hermes 3000 that
> Blumenberg left. He supposed it had been provided for that
> purpose—it was nearly new, and Blumenberg himself preferred
> charcoal or India ink. The ribbon was black. The Hermes had a
> pleasing gray-green tint, and only after three days did Potter come
> to understand the case to be plastic, not metal. This was the first
> such portable he'd used, and the small precise shapes of the letters
> looked like print. It had elite type. He took comfort in that.
> Blumenberg must have wanted him to feel at home—he'd amassed
> all the needful supplies. The sculptor hoped his assistant might
> remain, it seemed, or could not keep his promise that the Coast
> Guard would arrive.

All these are minor adjustments, and it's not clear that the final version improves upon the first (which had been often revised as well, when composed to start with). The shift from first to third person does count, and so does the shift in tenses, but the feel of the passage remains much the same. It's more important to consider larger questions—do the first lines engage attention, is there sufficient detail to interest but not bore the reader, is there something somehow at stake? These are the questions every author asks, or should, at some stage of a book's construction, and I use my own abandoned effort as example not because I think it exemplary but because I feel entitled to "mess" with the language and question the construct in this particular way.

In his masterful novel *La Peste* (*The Plague,* 1947), Albert Camus creates a character, Joseph Grand, who dreams of composing a fiction that will be his life's crowning work. All through the plague that ravages the North African town of Oran, Grand labors at the book's first sentence, trying to get it just right. The publishing powers in Paris, he hopes, will gather at a polished table and, having opened his manuscript, breathe a collective sigh of admiration and declare, *Chapeau!* Hats off, they'd say, we're in the presence of greatness; gentlemen, let's publish his wonderful book!

For years and years this modest functionary has struggled with that first sentence, composing it over and over while dreaming of perfection. At length he dies of the plague. Then Dr. Rieux—the central character in *La Peste*—goes to Grand's apartment only to find innumerable versions of that opening line and no second sentence at all. Camus may well have been referring to Gustave

Flaubert's quest for *le mot juste,* the perfect word, the exact choice of adjective, adverb, noun, and verb. Or he may have been referring to the larger matter of absurdity—the Sisyphean labor of cresting a hill while pushing a rock, only to lose purchase and watch the boulder roll away. And then to start again. But there's no more telling image of a would-be novelist wrestling with the demons of creation and failing, failing utterly, to pin the sentence down.

Some writers follow that model—working and reworking prose until they can continue with the draft. Others promise themselves they will polish the parts once the whole has been roughed in. Still others find a middle way and refashion what they've written, but not obsessively, and add to that first sentence. The opening does matter, since it establishes tone. However the writer elects to proceed ("Call me Ishmael," or "Call me, Ishmael"), the terms of engagement and rules of the game have been set.

No first sentence is impossible. Some opening lines, of course, are more possible than others. But the writer is the literal lord of a fictive domain, and can begin wherever she wants. By the second sentence, however, there's a reduction of possibility; you can't shift tone or diction at will, and must follow your own rules. If you start with a first-person present-tense voice ("I write this from the island . . .") you can't shift to third-person past tense on the very next page. If your first locale is rural, you can't move to a city in the second paragraph. Unless, of course, your topic is disorientation or, in the larger sense, disjunction—in which case such shifting might make sense.

This delimiting process continues, until by the close of the book all alternatives have been eliminated and there can be only one final line: the piece of a puzzle completing the whole. Other options will have been eliminated, and the precedent rules still apply. Whatever your "origin story," it carries through to the end.

Flannery O'Connor was, I think, a true original. So were Jane Austen and Emily Dickinson, and it's not an accident that each was a woman. Though scarcely unlettered or ill-schooled (indeed, the most recent of the trio, Ms. O'Connor, attended the Iowa Writers' Workshop and received an MFA), they were private in their practice and worked in solitude. It's only in quite recent times that the idea of a literary "sisterhood" has grown widespread and commercial; for far more of our history, the gifted female writer was expected to "go it alone."

One could even argue that a preeminent female author of the early twentieth century, Virginia Woolf, attained her place in part because of a supportive circle of fellow artists in what we now call the Bloomsbury group; further, she had the unstinting aid of her husband, Leonard, and they were not poor. (Another writer, Shirley Jackson—married to the Stanley Edgar Hyman of whom I write in Chapter 1—is much more widely read today than was the case when alive.) Almost without exception, those women whom we honor as successful early authors—Marie de France, Eleanor of Aquitaine, and, plausibly, Lady Murasaki or Sappho—were amateurs and privileged, not scrambling for a living or on the Grubstreet streets.

In *A Room of One's Own* (1929), Woolf makes an indelible case for equivalency and entitlement for "common" or "middle-class" women; until then, as with "Shakespeare's sister," there had been no traveled road to recognition as a writer. In her series of lectures at Girton College, she recounts in coruscating if imagined detail what might have happened to "Judith," Shakespeare's sister, who was born with the same splendid gift. Though every bit her brother's equal in talent, she would not have had a career. Judith would have profited neither from schooling nor the support of her parents, who expected her to marry a local yokel and renounce all thought of art:

> She could get no training in her craft. Could she even seek her dinner in a tavern or roam the streets at midnight? Yet her genius was for fiction and lusted to feed abundantly upon the lives of men and women and the study of their ways. At last—for she was very young, oddly like Shakespeare the poet in her face, with the same grey eyes and rounded brows—at last Nick Greene the actor-manager took pity on her; she found herself with child by that gentleman and so—who shall measure the heat and violence of the poet's heart when caught and tangled in a woman's body?—killed herself one winter's night and lies buried at some cross-roads where the omnibuses now stop outside the Elephant and Castle.

Such a scenario is grim but no doubt accurate; I know of no early instance of a woman escaping poverty by virtue of her pen. By the time of Fanny Trollope and "the lady novelists" of the late nineteenth century, this was no longer impossible or, at any rate, improbable. Today the bars of gender and color are less rigid and exclusionary, and those who earn prizes or best-seller status are often as not female. But the chance to work in Joyce's "silence, exile, and cunning" may have enhanced and not diminished the chances of originality; the three women I named at the start of this passage (Austen, Dickinson, O'Connor) spawn legions in their wake. Those who once worked in privacy are public figures now.

❧

Overheard at the Fifth Avenue parade: "Look, Mabel, my Johnny's the only one in step!" That "different drummer" of whom Thoreau wrote is often if not always out of step with his or her compatriots; the black sheep in the herd of white, the stranger in a crowd. Yet it's not necessarily true that the outlier or contrarian is worth the watching or listening to; to call a person "one of a kind" feels double-edged. Depending on intonation, the phrase may be a compliment or insult; context is all.

Take criminal behavior. The mass murderer or sociopath is routinely described as a "loner" raging against societal norms. Indeed the term can be employed as a legal defense for those whose behavior is aberrant, and it's one of the ways in which genius and madness may be made to seem akin. Transgressive action can be self-destructive as well as destructive of others, and psychological derangement (as with the poets John Clare, Friedrich Hölderlin, or Arthur Rimbaud) is nearly commonplace. François Villon and Jean Genet—the former in the fifteenth century, the latter five hundred years later—are honored in part not despite but because of their having been jailed. Entertainers are habitually celebrated for hard-drinking, drug-taking excess, and the greater the risks run, the larger the reputation. To die young or as a suicide is—I write this tongue-in-cheek, of course—a canny career move; my imagined sculptor, Blumenberg, trebled the value of his work once dead and washed ashore.

In terms of art, however, to have an "original" vision is almost always praiseworthy, if only long after the fact. Most writers we read and admire were once construed as ground-breakers, iconoclasts, or some other label for against-the-grain inventiveness; the writer who stays within and codifies accepted practice seems somehow less admirable than the one who strays. This is a case by case circumstance and shaky general assertion, but it nonetheless feels fair to say that we as a culture exalt innovation and those who break the rules. Or those who look afresh and with innocent eyes. Take the celebrated example of Saint-Exupéry's *Le Petit Prince,* where a hat on the ground looks, to the prince, like a boa constrictor digesting an elephant. All adults reading the story construe it to be a familiar shape and simply a piece of apparel; to the child—who sees with his heart, not eyes—the snake and swallowed pachyderm come clear.

In the visual arts such "ways of seeing"—to borrow a phrase from the critic John Berger—can be physical or physiological as well as creative or willed. El Greco's elongated figures and mannerist gestures may have been a simple function of astigmatism; had the artist worn glasses with the correct remedial prescription, his *Christ Healing the Blind* or *View of Toledo* might not have seemed extreme. What looks contorted to a modern eye may have been, to El Greco, a realistic representation of the body or sky under stress. Had Claude Monet's vision not degenerated over time, we might not have had the series of water lilies collectively known as *Nymphéas;* his luminous delineations of the pond behind his house owe at least a little to the cataracts that afflicted the artist in old age. Jackson Pollock's reputation rests almost wholly on his action paintings, which have no obvious precedent; the stage-by-stage preliminaries (from his years as a student of Thomas Hart Benton's through his experiments in abstract expressionism) now seem derivative. It's as though he were born with a dripping paintbrush and overflowing can of paint in hand, but in fact the "great leap forward" had been practiced step by step.

In music much the same holds true. Arnold Schoenberg and Duke Ellington, to name just two of the "originals" of twentieth-century composition, made experimental innovations in a system established earlier. The blind Ray Charles or the jazz masters Charlie Parker and Charles Mingus each had antecedents, and it takes nothing away from their startling-seeming originality to know it took time to mature. Beethoven's late string quartets, we think, owe their other-worldly dissonance to the composer's failed hearing; when he lost all aural connection to the "outer" world, "inner" harmonies came clear. These are well-worn and widely cited examples of the linkage between ordinary limitation and extraordinary expressiveness, both of eye and ear.

Good fences make good neighbors, yes, but borders are meant to be crossed.

Our modes of artistic expression have altered over time. It's clear the center of literary energy no longer resides in the poem, play, or novel—those dominant forms of the past. Where once the young man or woman hoped to be a playwright, she or he aspires to be a screenwriter; where once the dream was of a published sonnet sequence, the goal now is of a Netflix contract, or a network sitcom.

My compatriots in college who wished to join the writers' trade were by and large engaged in writing poetry or prose; for this year's crop of graduates a screenplay or original television series is the hoped-for prize. The "moving picture" and the TV set could not have been imagined in the nineteenth century, and today's technology will in the future no doubt seem archaic and be in turn replaced. The word *original,* so central to this chapter, pertains to these forms of expression, even if and when they seem derivative: there's something new under the sun . . .

Much of this has to do with the nature of the audience: incomparably larger in the mass-market fields. Take all the best-sellers published this year on the *New York Times* Best-Sellers List for fiction and add them up and compare them to sales figures for a "blockbuster" movie. The economy of scale here makes such a tally laughable: the film's yield will be a giant to the writer's pygmy, and if quantity not quality is the standard, there's no comparison. One hundred million dollars is a not-uncommon box-office sum in the first weekend of distribution of a major motion picture, but no text in publishing history has come remotely close. And poetry books (although sales are on the increase) remain a minuscule component of the market. So the stakes are far, far higher in the game of entertainment, and to the degree that the young artist plays the game of "risk-reward," it's likely he or she will opt for those more modern and commercial modes.

Attention span matters as well. To write a large-scale novel is to commit to the project for years; to read it is to consign many hours or days or even weeks to the task. As we're often reminded, however, the pace of our current way of life has grown more rapid and sporadic; the creative personality has less uninterrupted time to spend in the service of art. So the thirty-minute television show, with its fifteen- or thirty-second-long series of advertisements, is better suited to and more representative of the speed of our consumer culture than, say, Anthony Powell's stately *A Dance to the Music of Time.*

Our elder daughter, Francesca, provides a case in point. After college, she earned an MFA degree in prose fiction and published a much-praised novel, *Ask Me Anything,* in 2004. Soon thereafter she moved to the West Coast and now is the co-creator (with her husband, Nicholas Stoller) and show-runner of a Netflix series *Friends from College.* I have asked Francesca to report on the difference between the two worlds and to describe the transition between what Dylan Thomas called "my craft or sullen art" and "the writer's room." Here are her thoughts:

> When I completed my MFA in writing in the spring of 2000, I remember leaving my last fiction writing workshop and going out for drinks with my classmates at our usual bar to toast how far we'd all come, how much work we'd accomplished in graduate school and how much we'd helped each other and grown close along the way. It was a celebratory night and a late one and we all drank too much and promised each other we'd keep in touch and keep reading each other's work and stay close as a community of writers, even as we scattered across the country to teach, to work in publishing, to plod away at our separate projects. And what I remember most clearly is trudging home from the bar, the night cold and the undergraduates rowdy, and thinking to myself: *shit. It's over now.*
>
> The truth, which I knew then but couldn't quite admit, was that workshop was always my favorite part of graduate school. I loved

sitting around that big conference table and debating with my classmates, I loved talking about books and essays and poems and movies and fighting over each other's manuscripts and advocating for different directions in the plot, different narrative strategies. So many of the writers in my fiction cohort were brilliant and funny and sharp and observant, and when they trained their eyes on my work it was terrifying, but it also felt like getting away with something—all of these incredible thinkers, giving me ideas and breaking open scenes and chapters and coming up with possibilities for my novel that I had never even thought of. It was thrilling. And it was social, and it was collaborative, and it was exhilarating, and it was fun. Which is not a word that I ever once used to describe the feeling of sitting alone in my silent apartment, day after day, staring at the computer screen and using any available excuse to hop up from my desk chair and do anything other than write. Boy did I talk with a lot of telemarketers in those years, there was no phone call I wouldn't answer . . .

The story of my path into television is too long to lay out, but what I've found in this new form is what I loved most about graduate school. All television writing staffs work differently, but they are inherently collaborative and social. The best writer's rooms, like the best MFA programs, are places where writers from different places with different kinds of education and life experience and training get together to focus their sense of story and character into a joint project. It's not a democracy, because the person who creates the show or who has been hired to run it has to make the decisions about what gets into the scripts and what doesn't. But it is still, effectively, many people using their best intelligence to make a piece of writing really work. Television scripts that bear the name of a single writer usually reflect the work of many participants on a writing staff: people who have helped come up with the story and the structure and the lines and the jokes. When things are working well, you have the momentum of ten writers (or eight, or sixteen, or four) building on each other's story ideas, second-guessing each other's instincts, kicking the tires on every single joke, every line, every turn in the plot. When things aren't working so well, you have ten writers to procrastinate with and to watch trailers online or talk about the morning's headlines or the week's election results, and you also have free lunch.

William Blake too was an "original." Here again the line of demarcation between genius and madness is an uncertain one. Few men were so abundantly gifted and very few so productive, but the prodigious achievement had attendant costs. As with Virginia Woolf, the artist's hold on diurnal reality was episodic and shaky; he went in and out of focus like a scratched or fogged-up lens. Both as a writer and painter he traveled where few others went; his vision was transgressive from the start. Again, the lack of formal schooling or codified apprenticeship may have helped not hindered Blake's imagination, for though he did have training in the printer's and the draughtsman's trade, he was by and large self-taught.

And his innovations were real. In a prospectus for one of his "illuminated" books, in 1793, he declared with proud immodesty:

> The Labours of the Artist, the Poet, the Musician have been proverbially attended by poverty and obscurity; this was never the fault of the Public, but was owing to a neglect of means to propagate such works as have wholly absorbed the Man of Genius. Even Milton and Shakespeare could not publish their own works. This difficulty has been obviated by the Author of the following productions now presented to the Public, who has invented a method of printing, both Letter-press and Engraving, in a style more ornamental, uniform, and grand than any before discovered, while it produces works at less than one fourth of the expense.

The third of seven children, the poet lived (except for three years in the village of Felpham) all his life in London. Blake was born in Soho in 1757; he died in Charing Cross in 1827, three months short of his seventieth birthday. Raised by a hosier of at-best-moderate means, he attended school only until the age of ten, then was apprenticed to the engraver James Basire of Queen Street for a period of seven years. Thereafter, he taught the trade to his devoted wife, Catherine. His illustrated books and his new "method of printing" are almost without precedent, though the illuminated manuscripts of the early Middle Ages may have proved predictive of *The Marriage of Heaven and Hell.* But the labor of anonymous monks is only a distant precursor of what Blake hoped would be a form of mass production, and modern technology has rendered his inventiveness redundant; he stands alone. Largely ignored in his lifetime, the artist's work is, as Northrop Frye observed, "in proportion to its merits the least read body of poetry in the English language." The brilliant prose and verse, the remarkable drawings and designs, the complex ideation and system of belief—all these were accomplished against daunting odds. What Blake achieved in his illuminated books—both technically in the marriage of engravings to color and script, and prophetically in the ideas propounded—goes beyond all easy understanding. *The Songs of Innocence, The Songs of Experience, The First Book of Urizen,* and the other Prophetic Books are dense with arcane allusion and private mythology, though he intended them to make clear sense to the untutored reader. As he put it, in his address to "the Christians" in *Jerusalem* (1804):

l give you the end of a golden string,
Only wind it into a ball:
It will lead you in at Heaven's gate,
Built in Jerusalem's wall.

The artist was quarrelsome, a contrarian; he fulminated against Sir Joshua Reynolds and the Royal Academy, although he studied in and did exhibit there. Emanuel Swedenborg had been an influence; Blake quarreled with him too. His views on religion, on married and free love, on politics and literature—all were in some degree scandalous: which is to say, advanced. That overused word "visionary" is wholly appropriate here. Though the language of the Bible and the art of Michelangelo can be claimed as influential, and though the politics of such men as Thomas Paine were influential also, there's no real antecedent for the work produced. From an early age Blake claimed to have had visions, and they organized his thinking as well as his art. Often he had seizures—what we now might call *grand mal.* Two siblings died in infancy, and as he wrote in a letter of condolence to a friend whose son had just died, "Thirteen years ago I lost a brother, and with his spirit I converse daily and hourly in the spirit, and see him in my remembrance, in the region of my imagination. I hear his advice, and even now write from his dictate."

Dismissed as "mad" in his lifetime, he has been resurrected since. The Romantic poet was much admired by the pre-Raphaelites and, closer to our own period, the 1950s Beats and those who, in the 1960s, embraced sexual liberation. That Dante Gabriel Rossetti, Algernon Charles Swinburne, Allen Ginsberg, and Bob Dylan should claim him as an influence gives some sense of Blake's "afterlife" and how his almost-total anonymity has turned to present fame.

❧

In *A History of Reading,* Alberto Manguel incisively discusses what we take to be the beginnings of that precursor to reading: the act of writing itself.

> In all probability, writing was invented for commercial reasons, to remember that a certain number of cattle belonged to a certain family, or were being transported to a certain place. A written sign served as a mnemonic device: a picture of an ox stood for an ox, to remind that reader that the transaction was in oxen, how many oxen, and perhaps the names of a buyer and seller. Memory, in this form, is also a document, the record of such a transaction.
>
> The inventor of the first written tablets may have realized the advantage these pieces of clay had over the holding memory in the brain; first, the amount of information storable on tablets was endless—one could go on producing tablets *ad infinitum,* while the brain's remembering capacity is limited; second, tablets did not require the presence of the memory-holder to retrieve information. Suddenly, something intangible—a number, an item of news, a thought, an order- -could be acquired without the physical presence of the message-giver; magically, it could be imagined, noted, and passed on across space and beyond time. Since the earliest vestiges of prehistoric civilization, human society had tried to overcome the obstacles of geography, the finality of death, the erosion of oblivion. With a single act—the incision of a figure on a clay table—that first anonymous writer suddenly succeeded in all these seemingly impossible feats.

Further:

> It would be hard to exaggerate the importance of the scribe's role in Mesopotamian society. Scribes were needed to send messages, to

convey news, to take down the king's orders, to register the laws, to note the astronomical data necessary for keeping the calendar, to calculate the required number of soldiers or workers or supplies or head of cattle, to keep track of financial and economic transactions, to record medical diagnoses and prescriptions, to accompany military expeditions and write dispatches and chronicles of war, to assess taxes, to draw contracts, to preserve the religious texts, and to entertain the people with readings from the epic of Gilgamesh.

All this, it should be noted—with the exception of the final four words—deals with the place of writing in the workaday world, and not with its honored position in the realm of art. Most readers now pay more attention to Gilgamesh, that strange and riveting epic poem, than they do to "financial and economic transactions" of the period in Babylon. At the time, however, as Manguel suggests, "the importance of the scribe's role" was only in small part creative. The primary historical function of the scribe had to do with dictation and transmission: a taking down of the language of others in the functions listed above. Only slowly and haltingly, over time, did the idea of writing come to be associated with that of the lone individual transcribing in some private place some private emotion or thoughts.

The very concept of the individual—a distinct entity within a group—is relatively new. Most activity was tribal or communal, and it took millennia before our species came to honor the act of personal expression as something set apart. The poet, with his "eye in a fine frenzy, rolling" is a figure of fun to Shakespeare (*Midsummer Night's Dream,* act 5, scene 1), and the image of the solitary man or woman writing her or his feelings and opinions down in silence is, in effect, romantic. It's no accident that the

Romantics, as we have come to call them, came center stage as late as the nineteenth century, when opposition to established norms had become acceptable. I mean by this that writers in their early incarnation were more often than not a part of the community and occupied a place—no matter how minor—in court.

Michel de Montaigne (1533–1592) is often hailed as our first "modern man." His *Essais* are remarkable, not least for their self-scrutiny, and in later years he covered a wide range of topics on the relation of the individual to society, topics such as "Of Sadness and Sorrow," "Of Pedantry," "Of Constancy," "Of the Affection of Fathers to Their Children," "Of Cannibals," "Of the Inconvenience of Greatness," and "Of Conference." There are more than a hundred such, and they offer up a portrait of the private man writ large. As the author Sarah Blakewell writes in her *How to Live, or A Life of Montaigne in One Question and Twenty Attempts at an Answer,* "Learning how to die was learning how to let go, learning how to live was learning to hang on."

It's worth remembering, however, that the author was a man of independent means, a member of the nobility with a tower to retire to, a personal library, the habit of leisure, and few competing tasks. As long ago as Socrates, we were informed, "An unexamined life is not worth living," but Socrates spoke and did not write those words; it took his student Plato to record them. The idea of introspection—and a written reportage thereof—is embodied in and by Montaigne. As he so cogently put it, "If I knew my own mind, I would not make essays. I would make decisions."

Perhaps the most famous use of a related word comes from a book discussed in Chapter 3. As suggested there, Charles Darwin's *On the Origin of Species* changed the way that *Homo sapiens* considers its own origin, and has forever altered how we think of ancestry and, as it were, originalism. This latter term has been coined by those who think our Founding Fathers were in all things irreproachable, and there are still a few believers in immutability. They say—in error, I believe—that nothing has changed or should change. But Darwin's daring proposition is that life (and, by extension, thought and art) evolves.

My point therefore comes down to this: original work is evolutionary and with antecedents, no matter how it vaunts itself as new. "Imitation" and "Originality"—the opposed-seeming terms of these chapters—are at their base conjoined. Most manifestos (think of Marinetti's *The Futurist Manifesto* or Gustav Klimt's *Vienna Secession*) claim that what they say or how they paint has not been said or imagined before. Often, the innovative artist stands in opposition to the reigning taste and fashion of the time. But progress is reactionary in the root sense of *reaction;* it requires an established system to oppose. Again, we're in the realm of Kant's "antinomies," where—in the colloquial usage—opposites attract. The thesis and antithesis that Marx defined as historical materialism is in this regard representative: the synthesis produced is something new until it in turn grows old.

From the philosophical point of view, total originality is incoherent to the point where it cannot be stated, because an object so new that it bears no comparison with others, or antecedents from which no evolution can be traced, would be one for which we have no language to give meaning to how it *is* new. To state the terms for newness is to do so only within similarities, where the "novel" part can be by adjacency described . . .

I'm aware that there are many names in the preceding paragraphs (Darwin, Kant, Klimt, Marinetti, Marx) and I list them to suggest the phenomenon's widespread. It takes little or nothing away from the concept of originality to suggest it too has origins and, in such a dialectic, each synthesis begins as thesis until it in turn is opposed. The "original" artist—Joyce, Woolf, Blake, et al.—breaks new ground, but on a trodden path. To go where none has gone before is to continue walking, working, for no explorer starts at journey's end.

7 more matter

My mother had an amateur's interest in graphology—the pseudo-science of handwriting analysis—and there were several books on the subject in our house. Omnivorous, I studied them, and with the logic of an eleven-year-old came to the conclusion that genius and illegibility were somehow akin. Though I can't claim the former of these attributes, the latter—illegibility—has been a hallmark of my writing ever since.

The thesis of graphology is that personality can be revealed by, say, the size of a letter or the slant of script; an emphatic downward stroke is revelatory, and a period or exclamation point tells us something consequential about the writer's character. An optimistic nature might display an up-ward-rising trajectory to the sentence on the page; a depressive would show the reverse. A backward-facing lean to the letters suggests a different kind of individual than does a forward-tilting one, and, no matter how we try to hide or even "forge" it, our script displays our mood.

There were illustrative plates: examples of the hand of eminent men such as Beethoven, Einstein, Napoleon, and, of course, John Hancock. This last-named signatory (because of his pride of place in the Declaration of Independence) has come to be a synonym for the word "signature" itself. "Put your John Hancock here," we say, inviting a stranger to sign. In my youth, I had a perhaps pre-cocious desire to be notable, and notability—it seemed to me—meant handwriting hard to decipher, like a physician's scrawl.

So I set about imitation. Leonardo da Vinci proved difficult to copy, since he was left-handed and used mirror-writing as a kind of code. Probably he wrote from right to left in his notebooks in order to avoid smudging the pages with ink. Reversing the proce-dure of a right-handed scribe, Leonardo let ink dry on his thoughts while continuing to record them on the page. Beethoven, Einstein, and the rest wrote left to right and had in common (in part, no doubt, because these two wrote in German) obscure lettering to parse. So I took *this* one's strong downward slash, *that* one's upward-facing flourish in a capital letter, *this* one's angularity and *that* one's emphasis on separation between the *d* and *e,* and soon enough my script too became illegible. When I could no longer read what I wrote, I put down my pen and felt like a genius too . . .

Before that, I'd been dutiful, practicing script on lined pages and following the Palmer Method, as we were taught in school. The Palmer Method was developed by Austin Palmer in the late 1880s and introduced by him in *The Palmer Method of Business Writing* (1894). The idea was to use the arm's proximate muscles rather than those of the fingers to guide the pencil or pen, and the claim—unfounded, no doubt—was that a scribe could equal and even outpace the speed of a standard typewriter. It succeeded the more laborious Spencerian Method of Writing, which had been an accepted teaching tool for fifty years; it was in turn succeeded by the Zaner-Bloser Method, which taught schoolchildren to form manuscript letters rather than write in cursive. Now the D'Nealian Method of handwriting—teaching both cursive and manuscript—has become the instructional vogue. We need not go into detail as to the distinctions here; some methods urge arm movements, wrist movements instead, or finger movements only, but each and all of them are in the service of uniformity, rapidity, and a clear legible "hand."

The organizing principle of cursive—sometimes called "script" or "longhand"—is that, by joining the letters and not lifting the pen, one can increase one's speed. Formal cursive joins each letter; informal cursive permits pen lifts and pauses between them. You have only to watch a child laboriously forming "print" and "block" words, then learning to do so more quickly, then writing without interruption, to chart the young scribe's learning curve. My own progress had been rapid, but then I studied graphology and decided to be brilliant and what had once been clear became an unreadable scrawl.

The history of handwriting is an evolving one. We are accustomed to the way that spoken language changes—a difference of emphasis, tonality, pronunciation—but the written mode alters as well. A scribe in the twelfth century would form letters in a manner as separate from the contemporary court stenographer's as is the sound of Chaucer's language from an airport announcement today. Punctuation was erratic, the distinction between capital and lowercase letters hard to parse. Spelling was variable, largely phonetic, and often the student would copy out language in a kind of shorthand—possibly to save time while transcribing what the teacher said, possibly to save on the expense of paper, that rare thing. In the earliest examples we have of written compositions, there were no spaces between letters; their placement varied too.

Here, once again, from Alberto Manguel:

> Because books were mainly read out loud, the letters that composed them did not need to be separated into phonetic unities, but were strung together in continuous sentences. The direction in which the eyes were supposed to follow these reels of letters varied from place to place and from age to age; the way we read a text today in the Western world—from left to right and from top to bottom—is by no means universal. Some scripts were read from right to left (Hebrew and Arabic), others in columns, from top to bottom (Chinese and Japanese); a few were read in pairs of vertical columns (Mayan); some had alternate lines read in opposite directions, back and forth—a method called *boustrophedon* . . .

All this meant and means that writing—in the sense of marks on a retentive surface—is not a standardized procedure. The electronic signature with which we ratify documents today would have been unimaginable a few years ago; the methodology of future communication no doubt will further evolve. What's constant or at least consistent in the history of writing is the hope and expectation that a thing once written down will be preserved and read. And even this loose definition—think of messages composed in code, or disappearing ink—is subject to revision; it's a malleable mode.

Some time ago, at her younger sister's first birthday party, our six-year-old granddaughter offered to make and put up a sign instructing the assembled guests how to dispose of their trash. It was a garden party—paper plates and cups, ice cream and cupcakes and the paraphernalia of celebration: hats, balloons and bottles of juice and hot-dogs on the grill. There were two garbage cans. Penelope has an artistic nature; she lettered carefully, colorfully, then scotch-taped a sheet to the cans. This is what she wrote:

CEEP THE
RTH CLYN
RYYOUS
RYDOOS
RYSIYCL

Her school is a progressive one, earnest in its desire to instruct its students how to salvage or at least preserve the planet. What she was writing, for those readers who might require translation, was: "Keep the Earth Clean. Re-use. Reduce. Recycle." When, however, my wife offered to help the six-year-old with spelling, she shook her curly head.

"No, grandma," she said. "I prefer best guess."

From June through September 2018, the Morgan Library and Museum of New York showed a selection from the extensive Pedro Corrêa do Lago Collection of autographs; the exhibition was called "The Magic of Handwriting." This phrase comes from a letter from Stefan Zweig to Rainer Maria Rilke, asking for the keepsake of inked pages from his friend. There were samples of the hand and signature of, among other authors named in this book, Jorge Luis Borges, Emily Dickinson, T. S. Eliot, Antoine de Saint-Exupéry, Gustave Flaubert, Ernest Hemingway, Franz Kafka, James Joyce, Marcel Proust, Oscar Wilde, and William Butler Yeats. There were samples, also, of the autographs of such notables as Charles Darwin, Albert Einstein, Dwight David Eisenhower, Benjamin Franklin, Sigmund Freud, Abraham Lincoln, Karl Marx, and Napoleon. To name two figures *not* as yet included in this text, there were sheets composed by Ernest Shackleton—small and pinched, as if he knew he must conserve paper while marooned by ice—and Grigori Rasputin—by contrast profligate and sizeable, as if the "Mad Monk's" character went on bold display. A letter from Mary Shelley to the authorities in Viareggio and Livorno (quoted in Chapter 8) was on display there too.

My principal reaction, as I wandered through the room, was gratitude that these small scraps and snippets of the past have been preserved. The world we now inhabit is incomparably more populous, and we produce more language on a daily basis than ever in our history before. But a Facebook posting or email exchange is evanescent, fleeting almost by design, and the likelihood of lastingness is slim. A note composed by Johann Wolfgang von Goethe in the final week of his life has small intrinsic conse-quence, but the very fact we have it is cause for celebration; his long-dead hand still hovers near the page . . .

❧

Henry David Thoreau (1817–1862), in *Walden, or Life in the Woods* (1854), makes the following claim:

> Books must be read as deliberately and reservedly as they were written. It is not enough even to be able to speak the language of that nation by which they are written, for there is a memorable interval between the spoken and the written language, the language heard and the language read. The one is commonly transitory, a sound, a tongue, a dialect merely, almost brutish, and we learn it unconsciously, like the brutes, of our mothers. The other is the maturity and experience of that; if this is our mother tongue, this is our father tongue, a reserved and select expression, too significant to be heard by the ear, which we must be born again in order to speak.

The distinction between "mother" and "father tongue" seems both inaccurate and invidious, but the general pronouncement makes good sense. Thoreau was a solitary man, after all, and spent more time in silence than speech. As he puts it, "However much we may admire the orator's occasional bursts of eloquence, the noblest written words are commonly as far behind or above the fleeting spoken language as the firmament with its stars is behind the clouds."

In our present moment, this distinction has increased. Few are so fluent as writers that a first draft suffices as finished thing; the methodology of composition has much to do with revision.

Nearly no work of verbal art these days—these years and decades—is composed without close editorial consideration; spontaneity seems less of a virtue in writing than in speech. (The "blog" may well disprove this claim, since one of its aims is to narrow the distance between the two modes and let the reader feel as though he/she is "listening in" to the thought process of the writer. Just look at how your neighbors—the boy in the stands at a baseball game, the girl on the opposite seat of a train—compose their prose in a rush. Those quick fingers on the keyboard of a smartphone don't often pause in composition, nor does spelling matter much. There are emojis, contractions, the substitution of U for "you," and so on and so forth; there's "auto-correct" to serve as simultaneous interpreter of what's tapped out headlong at speed. A "tweet" is understood to be rapid and, as its name suggests, brief. It's also true that copy-editing has been devalued—even eliminated—by many publications, as if the accuracy of syntax and spelling feels less important now. But by and large the distinction does hold; we pay repeated attention to what we write and less to what we say.)

An additional mode shift attaches to this. With the substitution of typing or word-processing for "writing," the pleasure of manuscript parsing (seeing a passage crossed out, a word substituted, a phrase inserted) is less and less available to the literary scholar. So we can't count the two or three or many revisions a writer these days makes. ("Makes these days?" "few or many revisions?" "the numberless revisions?") Much language produced in the contemporary moment is written to start with on a computer, and drafts cannot be easily scrutinized for additions or deletions.

In this regard a first draft too may have multiple versions to scan. The "track changes" application is useful in the period of composition and editing, but it won't help a future doctoral candidate or would-be biographer to enter the mind of a writer at work. What we have are finished products, not the process on display.

It's worth remembering, further, that the history of writing and reading did not begin as a private or voiceless enterprise. The notion of an artist at work in splendid isolation, in an ivory tower or wooded retreat, is a modern one. In the scriptorium of medieval monasteries—literally "the writing room"—more than one scribe would share the space, and if they did so in silence it would be because of governing tenets of behavior that endorsed such silence. But the production of manuscripts was a communal procedure; the parchment and the inks and pens—as well as the task of copying—were shared.

So too is the idea of "silent reading" a relatively recent thing, and against the original grain. Perhaps because of the scarcity of books, as well as the relative paucity of those who were able to read them, the habit of reading began as an oral and aural affair. It still happens that a "designated reader" will sit at the head of a space—a room full of men cutting tobacco and rolling cigars, for instance—and read to the assembly from that day's newspaper or an agreed-on text. In those schools where textbooks must be shared, the lessons are spelled out aloud. And recitation in unison—call and response in houses of worship, or our classroom Pledge of Allegiance—is not uncommon today. In each act of silent reading, there's a precursor or presage of sound. "Sound it out," we tell the young reader, "and you'll hear what you see."

The modernist "masters"—think of James Joyce or Jorge Luis Borges, those two near-blind exemplars of literary excellence—would not have dreamed of first-draft publication; it's an axiom of all creative writing classes that a draft can be rewritten. At most we call it "work-in-progress," and the assumption is that progress consists of revision, a buffed-up-polishing of poetry and prose. Homer and Shakespeare, we suspect, did little of this; neither did George Eliot or Elizabeth Gaskell, but the contemporary author takes for granted that her or his expressiveness is something to monitor closely and, in the act of rewriting, improve.

This wasn't always the case. Those who once laid claim to education were schooled in the *trivium*—the study of grammar, logic, and rhetoric. Its Latin root means, in effect, "the place where three roads meet," and though it might stand lower as a course of study than the upper division of the liberal arts, the medieval *quadrivium*—arithmetic, geometry, music, and astronomy—the *trivium*'s skillset required attention. Once mastered, its techniques would be pressed into daily service in the writing of letters, essays, tracts, diaries, and books. One gets the sense that authors of the eighteenth or the nineteenth century did not need to disentangle their lines or struggle to make verb and noun conform. It's less a matter of natural facility than acquired skill, but prolific authors of the past seem more or less wholly confident that a sentence, once begun, will reach its appropriate end.

We've lost that confidence now. There are still, of course, exceptions to the rule. I think, for example, of the late Christopher Hitchens, who was rumored to have composed his articles at improvisational speed. Or Stephen King and Joyce Carol Oates, whose massive literary output cannot be apprehended except in terms of fluency. But most present-day authors labor over language in a way one imagines our predecessors did not. In their introduction to the First Folio of Shakespeare, in 1623, John Heminges and Henry Condell wrote admiringly of their dead colleague: "and what he thought he uttered with that easiness that we have scarce received from him a blot in his papers." The playwright Ben Jonson, reading this, is reported to have said in envious exasperation, "Would he had blotted a thousand!" To rest content with a first formulation is a gift given to few.

Let me belabor the obvious; writing comes in many forms. This book could have been focused solely on devotional prose, or on hagiography; it could have limited itself to philosophy or history, to the diary or journal mode, to scientific or technical writing, to biography or autobiography, to travel writing or children's books or comic books or picture books or nature writing or the exchange of letters between family members or lovers or rivals or friends. It could have dealt with writing not intended to be published or with writing tailored to an audience, that audience narrow or wide. There is contractual language, medical language, the language of instruction manuals or business proposals or cookbooks or merger agreements or marriage or divorce; there is legal language, ghetto language, the language of folk songs or jazz.

And within each form or genre there's wide range. The verbal play of Oscar Hammerstein or Stephen Sondheim and the "gangsta rap" of Jay-Z or Eminem share a mode of expression but little else; this is not to rank the writers but to point out how all-inclusive is the category "lyricist." The rubric "poetry" can describe the work engaged in by John Greenleaf Whittier or the alliterative verse of Cynwulf or the rhyming couplets of a Hallmark card. The genre "novel" can expansively include the work of Jane Austen and George Meredith or *Fifty Shades of Grey.* To say *A Better Mousetrap* and *King Lear* are both works of drama is only to say the form's elastic; what *Antigone* and *Jersey Boys* have in common is that both take place upon a stage.

Further, and crucially, there's a distinction between writing badly or well. If the title of this text were *Why Good Writing Matters,* it would have been far simpler to compose. One measure of a culture is its degree of literacy, its level of articulate expression, and to the degree that level declines, the culture is debased. In 1970, the journalist William Safire gave the then-vice president Spiro T. Agnew a now-famous phrase with which to attack his opponents in a speech: "nattering nabobs of negativism." Safire meant to mock the journalism establishment, and he did so alliteratively, with ten syllables in four words—at least one of which entailed a dictionary search. (The Merriam-Webster definition of "nabobs" is "a provincial governor of the Mogul Empire in India," and it has come to mean "a person of great wealth or high privilege.") The erudite journalist was writing tongue-in-cheek, perhaps, but Agnew used the phrase repeatedly, and it became a sort of slogan—widely understood by those who heard it as a verbal assault on members of the press. Now, half a century later, we repeat the dissyllabic phrase "fake news." As Hamlet says when comparing his father and uncle, "What a falling-off was there!"

I don't mean by this that "nattering nabobs of negativism" is a more memorable formulation than its present-day equivalent, but the rhetorical gap yawns wide. There's been a lowering of expectation, a sense that "polysyllabic utterance" is less appropriate as language than the far simpler "big words." As suggested elsewhere, one of the virtues of English is its all-embracing inclusiveness; an Anglo-Saxon word sits cater-corner to a Latinate one in almost every paragraph, and we borrow from Sanskrit or Urdu or Swahili with no sense that the "appropriation" is anything other than "appropriate." Our verbal ancestry is a mixed marriage—old English wed to court Latin after the Norman invasion of Guillaume le Conquérant in 1066—and the alliance of the Germanic and Romance language families has been a happy one.

Think of the dying words of Hamlet to Horatio: "absent thee from felicity a while, and in this harsh world draw thy breath in pain" (act 5, scene 2). There are two terms derived from Latin—*absentia, felicitates*—and twelve straight monosyllables while the Prince gasps for breath. Or, from Macbeth: "No, this my hand will rather the multitudinous seas incarnadine, making the green one red" (act 2, scene 2). The two elaborate words here—*multitudinous, incarnadine*—belong to a different verbal set than the straightforward rest of the language, but the great glory of the phrase resides in the dramatic yoking of the two. The Bard of Avon mastered, in unequaled fashion, this multiplicity of tongues within a single discourse; he's just as much at ease with the vocabulary of courtiers and kings as with that of tinkers and tailors, and his poems and plays resound with verbal juxtapositions such as those quoted above. A blind theatergoer at the Globe would have known—with no sight of the actors or their costumes—the social standing of a character just from the language and accent deployed.

Each of us has had a teacher; all of us are students. Whether home-schooled or in charter school, parochial or public, private or military, every American man, woman, and child has—or is supposed to have—access to education. Those societies that keep their citizens illiterate are backward-facing, barbarous, and the surest way to remedy intolerance is to encourage "book learning."

I have spent my life in school, first as a student, then teacher. We only rarely offer classes now in penmanship or how to diagram a sentence, but the writing of poems and stories is sanctioned in the syllabus. Things change. And though there are those who question it, it seems to me inarguable that such a course of study yields positive results. We do ourselves no damage by attending to our rhetoric; the reverse is also true. Inaccurate language, whether critical or creative, can do actual harm. When we fail to attend to precision and the truth of discourse, we put community at risk.

Our Founding Fathers were, almost without exception, a learned and literate crew. The letters of John Adams, Alexander Hamilton, and James Madison should give present authors pause; their command of political discourse stays more or less unmatched. Thomas Jefferson designed the University of Virginia and Benjamin Franklin sponsored the idea of lending libraries because an educated populace was necessary, they believed, to a functioning democracy. And today the ideal of universal literacy, though far from achieved, is widespread: a part of our national creed.

At present in America, however, our language is under assault. *I didn't say that,* we declare, or *I didn't mean to, not really,* or *I've changed my mind.* The president says something, then unsays it the next day. At his July 16, 2018, news conference with Vladimir Putin in Helsinki, for example, he made an assertion ("I would . . .") then reversed it by announcing he had been confused by the double negative and intended to say, "I would not . . ." Hyperbole and boastfulness are his chosen modes. His principal speech pattern is repetition, as if asseveration might make a falsehood true. He claims he has no time to read and books are an irrelevance to what he claims to know.

The Roman playwright Plautus, in his *Miles Gloriosus,* made a comic figure out of the "Braggart Warrior," and the play was turned, millennia later, into *A Funny Thing Happened on the Way to the Forum.* But when such braggadocio gains currency as political pronouncement, it is no longer amusing. Lie after lie accumulates, from early in the morning until late at night. The Greeks too had a word for it; an *alazon* is a person characterized by arrogance, boastfulness, a lack of self-awareness. *I would* and *I would not* do not mean the same thing.

Too, what holds true for public speech feels all the more disconcerting when composed in print. Remember all those candidates for public office or the judiciary who get caught and pilloried for what they wrote long years before, in an unguarded outburst or a candid moment. When a screed appears that slants or distorts the actuality of things, and is widely distributed and believed, we're in the realm of propaganda and "truthiness," not truth. (One of the president's lawyers, Rudolph Giuliani, went so far as to declare in public on August 20, 2018, that "Truth isn't truth"!) The whole apparatus of rumor-mongering and planted stories and undocumented assertions has harmed—I hope not fatally—the governing assumption that people mean what they write. This is why false claims and repeated lies and plagiarism are serious not trivial matters; when the misuse of language is intentional, democracy's under assault.

Imagine if the Declaration of Independence, one of our crucial documents, had been left unsigned. Imagine if the Gettysburg Address had been improvised by its author, and not jotted down or preserved. Imagine, further, that politicians might admit in private what they do not say in public (by now a near-daily occurrence) and get caught because the private utterance is revealed as an email or tweet. One can walk back a spoken phrase but less so what one writes. A line once set and printed claims a kind of perpetuity, at least until crossed out.

The Bulwer Lytton Fiction Contest has been established in order to honor the opening sentence of "the worst of all possible novels." Bulwer-Lytton himself began *Paul Clifford* (1830) with "It was a dark and stormy night," and the phrase has come to stand for a certain kind of literary excess and cliché. The sentence continues: "the rain fell in torrents—except at occasional intervals, when it was checked by a violent gust of wind which swept up the streets (for it is in London that our scene lies), rattling along the housetops, and fiercely agitating the scanty flame of the lamps that struggled against the darkness . . ."

This doesn't seem all that awful to me, at least in terms of scene setting and a mood evoked. The Bulwer Lytton contest invites its entrants, however, to do their worst. Since 1982 they have been doing so, often to true comic effect, but their *intention* is to write badly, and to my mind the comedy's increased when inadvertent. Famously the opening beat of *Irene Iddesleigh,* a novel published by Amanda McKittrick Ros in 1897, set the bar for the "worst novel ever written." Though there are many candidates, this one has been ranked as such almost from the date of publication:

> Sympathise with me, indeed! Ah, no! Cast your sympathy on the chill waste of troubled waters; fling it on the oases of futurity, dash it against the rock of gossip, better still, allow it to remain with the false and faithless bosom of buried scorn.

The examples of bad or inaccurate prose are legion, and it's shooting at clay pigeons or fishing in a barrel to compile a list. But here (under the general rubric "We must never let newspapers die") are a few headlines that seem apt:

Homicide Victims Rarely Talk to Police
Miracle Cure Kills Fifth Victim
Bridges Help People Cross Rivers
City Unsure Why the Sewer Smells
Man Accused of Killing Lawyer Receives a New Attorney
Federal Agents Raid Gun Shop, Find Weapons
Diana Was Still Alive Hours before She Died
Meeting on Open Meetings Is Closed
Statistics Show That Teen Pregnancy Drops off Significantly after
    Age 25

Perhaps I should have written "shooting at clay fishing" or "pigeons in a barrel," in order to announce the metaphoric mash-up of those lines. And, as all teachers know, it's rarely this amusing to encounter inaccurate prose. We spend much of our time correcting spelling, grammar, diction; we spend many of our reading hours wishing the reading were done. It's as though an oenophile and connoisseur of excellent wine were doomed to drink gallons of rotgut from a cardboard box. Bad writing is everywhere—*ubiquitous, omnipresent*—and at the risk of repetition or, more formally, palilogy, I'll say so again: bad writing is everywhere—*ubiquitous, omnipresent*—and a section on howlers could take twenty times as long.

But a line such as "I stood above a bottomless pit," is more than merely silly; it is, I'd argue, dangerous. There's no such thing as "a bottomless pit," and if there were, you surely couldn't stand "above it" but would fall. To say "They lived happily ever after" is less offensive, no doubt, but equally a fairy tale: untrue. From such small inaccuracies come large ones, and soon enough the failure of precision permits outright distortion and a tissue of lies like *Mein Kampf.* Our language is a precious resource, therefore one that can be fouled.

My great good friend and sometime editor Jim Landis (for many years the editorial director of William Morrow), compiled the earlier list of headlines as well as remarks about the profession and by professional authors. These, with his permission, come from his "commonplace book":

> "A writer is somebody for whom writing is more difficult than it is for other people."—Thomas Mann

"Writing is the only profession where no one considers you ridiculous if you earn no money."—Jules Renard

"First you're an unknown. Then you write one book and you move up to obscurity."—Martin Myers

"All that Mankind has done, thought, gained or been: it is lying as in magic preservation in the pages of books. They are the chosen possessions of man."—Thomas Carlyle

"The man who does not read good books has no advantage over the man who can't read them."—Mark Twain

"I'm a lousy writer; a helluva lot of people have got lousy taste."—Grace Metalious

"It took me fifteen years to discover I had no talent as a writer, but I couldn't give it up because by that time I was too famous."—Robert Benchley

"People do not deserve to have good writing, they are so pleased with bad."—Emerson

"Literature is an occupation in which you have to keep proving your talent to people who have none."—Jules Renard

"There are three rules for writing the novel. Unfortunately, no one knows what they are."—W. Somerset Maugham

"I write when I'm inspired, and I see to it that I'm inspired at nine o'clock every morning."—Peter De Vries

"A good writer is not, per se, a good book critic. No more than a good drunk is automatically a good bartender."—Jim Bishop

"When a man publishes a book, there are so many stupid things said that he declares he'll never do it again. The praise is almost always worse than the criticism."—Sherwood Anderson

"Some editors are failed writers, but so are most writers."—T. S. Eliot

"It's a damn good story. If you have any comments, write them on the back of a check."—Erle Stanley Gardner, to an editor

"Literature is mostly about sex and not much about having children, and life is the other way around."—David Lodge

An invented language, Esperanto, was conceived of and created by L. L. Zamenhof, a Polish Jewish ophthalmologist in the late nineteenth century. He made portmanteau words and simplified spelling central to the project; his ideal was that of universal speech. The aim of common parlance has had supporters since that time, but never gained true footing or took important hold. It seems—to those of us who revel in the richness and the tonal range of English—to be cutting off a nose to spite a face. To espouse phonetic spelling and a back-to-basics "universal language" is to strip our mother tongue of its beautiful complexity and settle for the lowest common denominator of discourse, not its inspired heights.

Nor does this richness and complexity, of course, apply to only English. The masterful French novelist Gustave Flaubert made precision his credo, cultivating *le mot juste*—the right word. The great German poet Rainer Maria Rilke wrote in his one extended work of fiction, *The Notebooks of Malte Laurids Brigge:* "Er war ein Dichter; das heisst, er hasste das Ungefähr." In my rough translation, this means: "He was a poet: which is to say, he hated the approximate." Or, perhaps, "He despised the inexact."

Art is exactness, the naming of names. When you call a spade a hoe or pitchfork, you do disservice to precision, and we require precision if we work with tools or label them in speech. The word "spade" has several meanings and multiple associations, and these distinctions must be noted when we call a spade a spade. As another major practitioner, George Orwell, wrote in his impassioned essay "Politics and the English Language," "The great enemy of clear language is insincerity. When there is a gap between one's real and one's declared aims, one turns as it were, instinctively, to long words and exhausted idioms, like a cuttlefish squirting out ink."

"I meant what I said and I said what I meant," is a chiasmus coined by Dr. Seuss in his *Horton Hatches the Egg*. (A chiasmus is a phrase in which central terms are reversed.) Then the rhyming line of the couplet completes the assertion, "An elephant's faithful one hundred per cent!" No clearer expression of fidelity to stated meaning seems necessary here; let it stand as a motto for all. The author of *Madame Bovary*, the arcane Symbolist poet, the political journalist, and the children's book author take the same position and espouse the same ideal. To mean what one says and to say what one means is the high charge of discourse—and all the more so, finally, when it's written down. Mark Twain, in his humorous vein, put it as follows: "The difference between the right word and almost the right word is the difference between lightning and the lightning bug."

In the last paragraphs I've cited five precepts from four different countries on accurate diction—from Gustave Flaubert, Rainer Maria Rilke, George Orwell, Dr. Seuss, and Mark Twain. The last three used pseudonyms; the authors were in actuality Eric Blair, Theodore Geisel, and Samuel Langhorne Clemens. Yet we know them by the pen names they used for publication—what's written has a permanence not available to speech. And that's perhaps the final yield of this business of writing; we keep them in the room with us, or on an airplane or beach. *Because* they wrote what we still read, they remain among the quick not dead; because their language was preserved in print, it instructs us still.

Henry James, in older age, spoke rather than wrote down his books. He dictated his lengthy, convoluted sentences first to his assistant William Macalpine and, later, to his amanuensis, Theodora Bosanquet. She was his secretary from 1907 till the year of his death, 1916. Trained in shorthand, she would sit in his study in Rye and copy out the tortuous tropes and complex subordinate clauses of the Master's considered and then reconsidered speech. In the garden room of Lamb House he recited and she wrote. To wit:

> The "Master" is the term by which his colleagues knew and called him, and the author did not disavow though rarely acknowledged that flattering term, since in some cloistered realm of self-regard he might well have construed himself thusly, and with a degree of justification, whereas the word amanuensis itself derives from the Latin for "by hand," and the no-doubt long suffering maiden lady—whom he called his "typewriter" and even his "Remington priestess"—did provide a kind of transcription for the workings of his subtle (at times over-subtle and delighting in parenthetical digression such as this one, or—"Try to be one of those on whom nothing is lost"—glancing observation, when at a certain hour the two took tea together, dedicated to that demanding enterprise also, this last phrase a paraphrase and even in small measure a parodic

echo of the opening sentence of his by-comparison youthful novel, *The Portrait of a Lady,* with its remarkable opening assertion that "Under certain circumstances there are few hours in life more agreeable than the hour dedicated to the ceremony known as afternoon tea," these lines composed and published in serial form in 1880 and then in the novel in 1881, and therefore long antecedent to, although he would revise it, his association with the aforementioned and above-named Miss Bosanquet, who herself would publish a memoir of her time with the great stylist, as well as several additional texts, not dying until eighty) mind. Punkt. Period. Full stop.

The tongue-in-cheek demonstration, above, of the way "the Master" worked, was a deal of fun to write if no doubt less so to read. It's a form of mimicry (or, more earnestly, mimesis) and an echo of the argument for "imitation" made in Chapters 2 and 5. I imagined the patient Miss Bosanquet sitting in the garden room—an extension of Lamb House in the village of Rye where Henry James was wont to pace and sound out his ponderous sentences—and felt sufficient sympathy for the constraint of her employment to try to make light of it, writing. The garden room itself was bombed in the Second World War, but his is a talkative ghost . . .

Long years ago, I wrote *Group Portrait: Conrad, Crane, Ford, James & Wells—A Study of Writers in Community* (1982). In order to research the locale of that community, I moved with my family to the area of the Cinque Ports—on the border of Kent and East Sussex—where the novelists once resided. It was still possible, although only barely, to meet residents of the region who'd been alive when my subjects lived there also, and on arrival I tracked several witnesses down. One old gentleman described

Joseph Conrad's behavior in the local barbershop and how he had very clean boots. "He was polite to me," averred my interlocutor. "And kind. I always think that kindness to young children is a mark of greatness. Don't you?"

This long-cherished memory did not, perhaps, enlarge my understanding of the novelist's aesthetic, but it brought the sailor-writer at least a little to life. Another witness, as a child in Rye, had been taken to Lamb House for tea, where she met "the Master." Salivating at the prospect of a personal encounter and remembered incident, I pressed her for whatever she recalled. This was in 1980; James had died sixty-four years previous, and she had engaged in "the ceremony known as afternoon tea" well before the First World War.

The elderly lady paused, recollecting. "Yes," she said. "I remember him well. He had a very loud voice."

Of such threads and scraps of anecdote do writers fashion their nests. The image of the ex-seaman Conrad "Jack-a-shore" with his well-polished boots, or the stentorian James, has stayed with me, and in the cap-tip here it surfaces again. A central thesis of this text is that just such mimicry enables the way we "learn" the world—allowing us, by way of example, to acquire fluency in a shared language. We stare at magicians or athletes in the attempt to follow their lead, trying in slow motion and then with incremental assurance to make a coin disappear or make a three-point shot or hit an overhead volley; why should we not attempt to copy artists too?

The writer's voice outlasts her or him; the authorial presence remains. Two days ago I attended a memorial service for a nonagenarian who'd been a passionate gardener; the event took place in his garden. There was music; there were people passing canapés and wine. There were personal remembrances, details of biography, a placard of photographs under a tent, and a leather-bound album to sign. All this was more or less standard procedure, but, at the end of the ceremony, a friend of the man we'd come to mourn recited the first verse of the dirge from Shakespeare's *Cymbeline:*

> Fear no more the heat o' the sun
> Nor the furious winter's rages
> Thou thy worldly task hast done,
> Home art gone, and ta'en thy wages:
> Golden lads and girls all must,
> As chimney sweepers, come to dust.

More than four hundred years have passed since those lines were composed; they still sound resoundingly. This also is "why writing matters"; at times of great emotion, elation, or solemnity we turn to touchstone rhymes and talismanic formulae and recite them to ourselves. They may be hokum: *This little piggy went to market;* they may be nonsense, *Abracadabra,* or shorthand: *R.I.P.* They may be grand and wishful, as in the last line of Cymbeline's dirge: "And renowned be thy grave!" But all of us have someone else's language in our head—a parent's advice, a lover's whispered endearment, an army sergeant's shouted drill—and when that language takes shape as something written down, it outlasts the speaker or writer and can be passed along. So, standing in the dead man's garden and hearing those six lines pronounced, I felt myself a part of long-standing tradition and was by the rhyming couplet consoled.

8 students

Picture yourself at a circular table of which there's no obvious center or head: the round table of *Morte d'Arthur*. Good King Arthur knew which of those who ate with him had merited proximity, a place at his right and left hand. Lancelot, Gawain? Tristan with his concubine, the fair Yseult? That large newcomer in green? What though the table was constructed to suggest equality, the knights well understood who sat "below the salt."

Or imagine yourself in a small room with desks arranged facing the window, and acolytes sitting on chairs. Is the position permanent or will you be replaced? Are you the leader or instead among the led? Do we take turns?

Most seminar rooms are cramped, and there was a time when such a space was smoke-filled, with ashtrays overflowing. Now often as not the walls are cinderblock and the window gives on nothing, and the desks are bare.

The procedure of teaching and learning—at least in this particular field—remains what it once was. Technological advance (cyber instruction, mass educational outreach, etc.) has little to do with the practice of writing, where the quill pen and the parchment sheet once seemed sufficient tools. A student still has much in common with her or his predecessors: the craft remains a matter of blackening the blank page. But how? But why? But when and where and for whom?

(1) Ten of us drove in a bus that held twelve: Susie, Helen, Jimmy, Paul, Dick, Richie, Evan, Barbara and me. And also, of course, Mr. Morse. He was driving and not happy with the rain. We sang camp songs and show songs and "Oh my Papa," which is what Eddie Fisher sang and made me want to cry. I sat between Evan and Paul. Richie's father owns a factory that makes a new kind of plastic sheet, a thing called polyethylene, and we had a roll of it in case the ground was wet.

Everything was wet. The windshield wipers slapped and slapped, and everywhere you looked were trees, and they were dripping. Saranac Lake was a long way away, and I had to take a pee and wanted to go home.

Maybe the rain would quit. Maybe the sun would shine. These were my classmates and I liked them, or anyway liked Paul and Richie and had slept over at his house but there was a moose by the side of the road and I want to go home.

Let's try again.

(2) A pilgrimage. Ten travelers drive in a bus that holds twelve: three girls, six boys—all adolescent, upper middle-class, white, their

hormones raging—and a teacher, the worried Dean Morse. The two rear seats are unoccupied—or, rather, piled high with gear. There are sleeping bags, back-packs, and cartons of food. There are sneakers and slickers and tents. Why, one wonders, does Mr. Morse teach; is it a genuine calling, a faute-de-mieux employment, an accident engendered by his parents' choice of name, so the academy has beckoned him from birth? In an earlier context—consider the novels of Anthony Trollope—the title "Dean" would have been church-related and not predictive of a high-school teacher's salary, the paltry $2,150.00 per annum that is his starting wage.

It is sufficient, however, for him to have proposed to Nellie last Thursday night, at dinner. She said Yes. She did so blushingly, becomingly, her hand on his right hand. "I love you very much," she said. "And that makes me very happy." They were eating snails.

One more time.

(3) Fuck it, fuck it, fuck it, why did I agree to this? I don't even like to swim. The tits on little Barbie-doll are going to be something, but they're not ready yet. And she's not ready yet. This campground sucks, the weather sucks, the kids are caterwauling camp-songs and I have three bags of marshmallows and five bags of potato chips and this shitty roll of plastic I have to spread by the fire and hope it doesn't catch. The plastic, I mean, not the fire; when Barbie comes over to help and leans over by the barbecue she shows me the crack of her ass. *The Scarlet Pimpernel* is what she wants to talk about, and I tell her, and mean it, it sucks.

Let's assume there are twelve students in the room. They have been given the same assignment: write about a camping trip when you were fourteen. Write about your friends, your fears, your teacher, the weather; write about what you know and if you don't know, make it up. Write from several points of view. This is the high charge of fiction, class: the way to move from reportage or fact-based remembrance to an invented yet recognizable world. *Here's* a mirror in your kit-bag, and *there's* surrounding nature; hold the mirror up.

Having drunk from their bottles of water or paper cups of coffee, the students set to work. They do so on their laptops, except for white-haired Muriel Palmer, who makes a show of penmanship—because of her last name, perhaps, the "Palmer Method"?—and uses a Montblanc.

Have you noticed, reader, that in the paragraph four paragraphs ago I made the same coy speculation as to the influence of names—in that previous instance not "Palmer" but "Dean"—and have you considered how many such names (Wheelwright, Boatwright, Carpenter, Smith . . .) do in fact describe professions? The twelve students have an hour to produce their compositions; they can revise, if they so choose, once class lets out. Lets them out. But the point of this particular exercise is to write to order, write *on* order, really, the way a scribe might copy down a letter spoken by an illiterate patron and sent by the speaker-purchaser home in order to offer up news. And have you noticed further, reader, that the notion of a scribe or perhaps amanuensis has been adduced or introduced in a previous chapter at small length? The aforementioned speaker and writer interchangeably inform those loved ones and family members left behind who no doubt are concerned to know how the wayfarer fares: his health, his job prospects, etc. Has he made friends, made good, made enough in the oil fields or mine fields or corn fields to send for his fiancée Clara and is she still available and does she want to come?

The scribe transcribes. He dips his pen in the glass bottle on the table, which holds ink. The bottle does, I mean, not table, for the latter holds or more accurately supports the former, and there are sheets of paper—these calibrated by quality, thickness, therefore price—and a single envelope with which at transaction's close to contain the folded and sealed and thereafter stamped whole. Paid for in rupees, dinars, dollars, dirhams, rubles, deutschmarks, lire, francs? The coin of which realm? At a fixed cost or variable, according to the length of the letter and time spent in dictation; is this a new or a regular customer? Will he, although analphabetic, write again next month?

And as long as we're discussing it, that's what Beckett did for Joyce—Sam, I mean, for his much-admired Irish uncle and godfather Jim, although there was no actual consanguinity or payment or, in the last analysis, influence, since Beckett, after his early and learned and, let's admit it, excessive inclusiveness (*vide Bellacqua* and *More Pricks Than Kicks*), as a prose stylist embraced simplicity, renunciation, excision, electing a language not his natal one because English was too easy (*idem* the eggs over easy in his long poem "Whoroscope") and writing thereafter in French, taking things out rather than putting them in—when the elder was too blind (not blind drunk, I mean, though that too happened every other Friday, but with his vision occluded) to write. "To be an artist is to fail where others do not dare to fail," as our modest yet arrogant boy would suggest. And that sexual suggestiveness (*vide idem* "taking things out rather than putting them in," as an emblem of parentheses and editorial intervention if not *coitus interruptus,* aren't we proud of our Latin?) is not inapposite, since there have been suggestions that Joyce's troubled daughter, Lucia, whom he all his life declared a genius though what she was was loony-tunes, had something of an affair with—perhaps on her part fantastical, imagined—or at least an interest in and expressed attraction to the tall and good-humored Irishman sitting opposite her father and taking dictation for *Finnegans Wake,* or so the story goes.

One fine afternoon in Paris there came a knock on the door, and Joyce called out, "Who's there?" It was the postman delivering a package and the addressee instructed him to "Leave it in the hall." Which words thereafter found their way into the manuscript because Beckett could not distinguish the dictation from the interruption, both of them after all verbal, and he bent over the page.

Where was Lucia when this happened, not to mention Nora Barnacle, her mother: were the two of them together in the kitchen making sandwiches, or in the bedroom and taking their ease on the patterned bedspread and propped up by soft pillows, the younger with spread legs, or out at market sampling goats' cheese or perhaps yesterday's bread? What did they talk of, the women: the weather, the price of suitably redolent *fromage du chèvre,* Michelangelo, the room? And when his amanuensis next session read the words spoken by and thence transcribed back to the senior author, Joyce said, "I didn't say that."

And Beckett insisted, "You did."

"All right," said J.J., acquiescent, "Leave it in."

A pleasant little canter that, a dainty trot. With so much more to say or write (the dark curls framing Lucia's face, the pointed nose, the yearning), the blue wool sweater Beckett wore, the cigarette smoke in the air. The passionate glance she wafts his way, the smoldering gaze, then downcast eyes, the crossed hands at her breasts. Doltish Giorgio, her brother, is not in the apartment but already with his drunken friends at a late lunch in the Brasserie Lipp; her mother is asleep and Daddums can't see anyway, so she could take those hands and fingers and one by one undo the mother-of-pearl buttons on her scented blouse, the tall Irishman watching, to reveal—epiphany!—the raised pink buds of her nipples beneath. It's less an invitation than a revelation, a promise of what might be his if only Beckett asked. Or took. There are those who maintain with certainty the at-best conjectural possibility that the pair did have a romantic encounter (although later the playwright denied it, denying in the face of her manifest mad misery that ever he took advantage of those spread legs on the rumpled bedspread referred to above, the high-piled pillows, the trembling fingers, the pale breasts, and anxious to preserve not so much his reputation as a rakehell as his welcome to her father's house, this being the master that young Sam craved and to whom he self-apprenticed, since after all the girl was stark raving, barking bonkers, hearing voices though not in fact his). "Leave it in the hall." So why would he risk a seduction—or, more properly, acceptance of what was on offer—if in such congress and the momentary spurt of pleasure or, if not pleasure, release and relief, he would thereby put at important risk the older writer's good opinion who was nothing if not jealous of his daughter's reputation and all his life defended her as a visionary, doubly sane, and not stark raving, barking bonkers, etc. Now if only half-envisioned and half-described as scene it must nonetheless stand as surrogate for all those scenes unwritten (Joyce and Beckett having breakfast, Joyce and Beckett taking tea, Joyce and Beckett in the Irish pub or as close as one can come to familiar flagrant Irishry on the left bank of the River Seine with its passing resemblance to and distant evocation of the River Liffey five miles meandering through Dublin—a smell of snails in garlic, fresh sawdust on the bistro floor—and telling Jewish jokes, the latter's accent atrocious but his timing good, the former breaking into song at his companion's urging or any provocation, really, since he is proud of his as-yet untenebrous tenor) because the hour's up. And class is over, class.

We meet again on Wednesday afternoon, one to three in the Senior Common Room. This time it's sunny, the curtains drawn wide, and the students sit together over lunch: soup, coffee, baloney sandwiches, cake. The paper plates and napkins and plastic forks and water bottles have been provided gratis. This second session follows the procedure of the first. Three more to come.

> (4) The wind is high. The waves of Saranac Lake, though not white-capped or dangerous, are nonetheless problematic for these inexpert children in their several canoes. One of them, Jimmy Levinsohn, has been to sailing camp and can handle his oar with assurance; Mr. Morse too feathers his paddle and knows how to steer. But the third and fourth boats wallow and, if not at risk of being capsized, make small headway in the wind. The wind is cold.

It's June 17, almost the start of the summer, yet the distant peaks of the now-not-so-distant Adirondacks still show forth, forebodingly, snow. And in any case the children have come unprepared for nature, they being Manhattanites all.

Red-haired and freckle-faced Susie sits in the prow of canoe #3, the orange one with splintering wood slats. She shivers; she's trying to enjoy herself because she knows she should enjoy herself but she is not, is nowhere near enjoying herself and wishes she were home. Home is where her stuffed wool bear still lies on her canopied bed, though when her friends sleep over she hides Winnie in the second drawer of her bedroom bureau because she doesn't want them to start teasing her or tell tales out of school. This is out of school with a vengeance—no houses she can see on shore, no motor boats on the water who could come to their assistance if they require assistance, and she doesn't want to think about it since she doesn't want to cry.

(5) If Nellie saw me now she'd laugh, or try to keep from laughing: the things we do for love. For love of golden Nellie I'm setting up a campsite on the shores of Saranac so as to earn—what, brownie points, approval?—from our revered and blessedly soon-to-retire principal Ed Tillar, who asked for volunteers. To chaperone this trip. When I raised my arm I knew he'd pick me since I'm in effect on probation, and the next three-year contract at Fieldston depends on my—what, deportment?—comportment with these children, only one or two of whom I like at all, and all of whom are spoiled.

But wouldn't it be wonderful to be up here with her instead, where Robert Louis Stevenson recovered from consumption, or attempted to, and wrote *The Master of Ballantrae,* or started to, and finished it in Vailima, where he died in the South Seas. To see it through her eyes. To see the Stevenson Cottage with Nellie on my arm. To escape these noisy children and their caterwauling camp songs and stand here in rapt silence with my fiancée instead.

(N.B. The Scottish author RLS in an effort to improve his health did in fact make a brief sojourn to, and on doctor's orders resided in, a sanatorium on Lake Saranac in 1887. He liked to sail. "The proudest moments of my life," he wrote, "have been passed in the stern-sheets of a boat with that romantic garment over my shoulders." He wrote this to W. E. Henley, the author of *Invictus* [1875], which begins, "Out of the night that covers me / Black as the pit, from pole to pole / I thank whatever gods may be / For my unconquerable soul.")

Which is neither here nor there.

(6) He insulted me. He turned away. He says he wants to go to Horace Mann instead, where they play better football and there are no girls. Well, he didn't say that thing about no girls but I know it's what he's thinking and I know he means it because he turned away. Mummy says I shouldn't let him kiss me because he'll make me pregnant and that'll be the end. I ask does kissing always make you pregnant? and she says, just wait and see. One thing leads to another, she says. I'm giving you a warning, girl, and you better listen, OK? When you start you just don't stop. It's best to just don't start.

"You all belong to a lost generation."

This is said by Auntie Gertrude with a wagging finger to young Ernie at her feet. Lately he wants to be Ernest, not Ernie, and though he is impressed by her—her massive calves, her close-cropped hair—he takes unkindly to instruction, always has. Well, that's not the whole truth, not really, he welcomes instruction from teachers and then says he taught himself. This is what he did with Fordie in the *Transatlantic Review.* This is what he did to Sherwood in the torrential spring. It's a complicated (notice the rhyme, class) thing. So when he nods in agreement and asks Miss Stein if he might copy out the phrase in the small notebook in his jacket pocket—her brilliant pronouncement, self-satisfied indictment of those who visit her *salon,* yet uttered with a fondness and hint of condescension, as though she were saying, "Oh, boys will be boys" and granting, in advance, absolution—she tells her protégé, "Yes."

You all belong to a lost generation, he writes. He is not, has never been good at spelling but gets the sentence right. And will use it for his epigraph—epitaph? epigram? what's the difference, why can't I remember?—in the book he's working on which soon will be complete about the sun. And then she says, "But Hemingway, remarks are not literature," and tells him to pour her more tea. An epigraph (a) sits at the start of the book, an epitaph (b) on a gravestone, an epigram (c) is a short and pithy saying that can in certain instances serve as an exemplum for either or both *a* and *b.*

It is 3:37 p.m. on September 24. The faded Persian carpet where he reclines full-length beneath her has tea stains on it, and cigarette ash, and red wine as well, but the cigarette ash is believed by Miss Toklas to be effective as a cleansing agent, and she rubs it patiently into the patterned carpet with her boot. They are both black-clad, these women, and late afternoon light through the window in the living room of the flat in rue de Fleurus accentuates their shared pallor: the one rotund and talkative, the other thin and silent, but somehow two peas in a pod. Since he has his pencil out, he writes this down as well, *somehow two peas in a pod.*

And then he writes: *ppod.*

The wall is bright with pictures, although several are dark. The pictures hang higgledy-piggledy, closely adjacent and with their frames touching: pencil sketches, charcoal sketches, watercolors, oils. There is Mr. Picasso and Mr. Matisse and Mr. Pissarro the Jew. Arising with some masculine difficulty from the floor where he lies sprawled—because between the footstool and the ottoman and piled books and paintings and the overstuffed chair his ditto hostess occupies there's insufficient space for a man already bulky and in any case not short but tall, broad-shouldered, and because he shadow-boxed before lunch and went three rounds with Morley, not to mention the writing that morning, not to mention the bed-bout with Hadley, not to mention the ache in his back—he goes to fetch the tea. He wishes it were wine. He wants to pour himself a brim-full glass from the decanter invitingly adjacent to the cheese board, but is mindful of his manners, not yet a regular in the *salon,* and wants to be invited again and therefore awaits her permission to drink.

"Un coup de rouge," she says.

Her accent is atrocious—even Hemingway can hear this—but the grammar is impeccable; she has lived in France for years. She is wealthy if not rich—not rich like Count Mippipopolous, not extravagantly so, but self-indulgent nonetheless in the acquisition of art. The pictures lean against the wall; they pile beneath the window seat; they cluster in the hall. They are landscapes and portraits and still lifes and studies of guitars. They are pictures she bought or was given and some that her brother owns too. He is heartily sick of the pictures and tea and thinks about Hadley in bed. He thinks about her hair and neck and thinks of quick little Callaghan weaving and bobbing and the left jab he perfected or, if not perfected, improved. Do not think I am impressed by this, but something in the way that Morley moved from side to side is good to pay attention to and then step forward to the right and so block off the ropes. That sentence he was working on—the one about the rainbow trout—is giving him the hell of a time, because although he got the trout he didn't get it right.

"Un coup de rouge," she says again, nodding, and now it is an invitation, and he returns to the sideboard and pours himself a glass. He lifts it in the fading light and takes a sample-sip. It tastes of cheese, it tastes of stables being cleaned and the stale whiff of hay. There are experts who admire this, who praise the taste of camembert and hay, but he is not an expert yet and has small *afición.*

If he were expert at tasting, he would spit it out.

Still, it is better than tea. Miss Stein and Miss Toklas have emptied the pot, and he can do likewise with the carafe, and so they return to the issue of syntax, the value of conjunctions, and, in effect, the grammatical equivalence of *and* and *or* or *but.* They discuss the distinction and if there *is* a distinction between polysyndeton and parataxis and which is more appropriate in English to deploy. When Scott arrives it's almost a relief. He comes in with McAlmon and they are being geniuses together and already two sheets to the wind. They clatter up the stairs and sit in chairs pulled out for them as if five make a party, *makes* a party, is it *make* or *makes?* and Callaghan kept jabbing with the left and then the right cross. Which he, Hem, did not see.

It was the *garagiste*'s remark, in fact, the one about being a lost generation, which Miss Stein repeated and had not been intended as literature but referring to the lack of knowledge about spark plugs and oil. How can I be your student when you know nothing of drive trains and axles and how they are connected and the feeling of things too is syntax if you would only pay attention, as at this moment Scott is most certainly *not* doing but instead is telling everyone about the bald bartender at the Crillon where they have had a drink, or three, or five, who mixes up olives and nuts. He has this rare disease, explains McAlmon, or perhaps it's a remarkable ability, but everything is synesthetic to the fellow who can't tell *blue* from the sound of an organ or *red* from the feel of a blanket, so why should we trust him, *in*-trust him with the mixing of martinis which arrive at your table with nuts?

Do not think I am impressed. Do not think I'll let that bantam Callaghan duck and weave that way again. Do not think I'll show Miss Stein this page or paragraph or line. Because, Miss Stein, she dead.

N.B. " 'Mistah Kurtz, he dead,' " is the line by Joseph Conrad near the close of *Heart of Darkness* and a submerged allusion here—too subtle, perhaps, by half. Necessitating identification if not elucidation, which is of course a shame. The same holds true for Edward Estlin Cummings, who wrote in *The Enormous Room* about the experience of driving an ambulance in the First World War (though focused on his subsequent incarceration in La Ferté-Macé), which experience could well be juxtaposed to that of the wounded novelist, and also coined—banked?—the quasi-famous phrase "since feeling is first / who pays any attention / to the syntax of things." Ditto with the referents to *The Sun Also Rises* and its epigraph and Count Mippipopolous and the memoir by Robert McAlmon, *Being Geniuses Together,* and the coy inclusion of Morley Callaghan and those people with initials, F. Scott Fitzgerald and Alice B. Toklas, etc. Not to mention the "masculine difficulty" referred to in *A Farewell to Arms* by E. H. "Will never wholly kiss you." Not to mention Stein.

❧

Two of my imagined dozen apprentice authors turn to the comfort of research and offer up the expertise of others. Why not? Lay down your weary pen, my love, and leave the rest to me. "Just the facts, ma'am," says Jack Webb.

This comes from Wikipedia, the Free Encyclopedia, though the entry is sixty years later than the scene described. I could, I suppose, return to the source and find a guidebook dated 1957, but why bother; this is fiction, is it not? And, in the realm of the imagined, things don't change.

> (7) Saranac Lake is a village in the state of New York, United States. As of the 2010 census, the population was 5,406. The village is named after Upper, Middle, and Lower Saranac Lakes, which are nearby. The village of Saranac Lake covers parts of three towns (Harrietstown, St. Armand, and North Elba) and two counties (Franklin and Essex). The county line is within two blocks of the center of the village. At the 2010 census, 3,897 village residents lived in Harrietstown, 1,367 lived in North Elba, and 142 lived in St. Armand. The village boundaries do not touch the shores of any of the three Saranac Lakes; Lower Saranac Lake, the nearest, is a half mile west of the village. The northern reaches of Lake Flower, which is a wide part of the Saranac River downstream from the three Saranac Lakes, lie within the village. The town of Saranac is an entirely separate entity, 33 miles (53 km) down the Saranac River to the northeast. The village lies within the boundaries of the Adirondack Park, 9 miles (14 km) west of Lake Placid. These two villages, along with nearby Tupper Lake, comprise what is known as the Tri-Lakes region.

Saranac Lake was named the best small town in New York State and ranked 11th in the United States in The 100 Best Small Towns in America. In 1998, the National Civic League named Saranac Lake an All-America City, and in 2006 the village was named one of the "Dozen Distinctive Destinations" by the National Trust for Historic Preservation. 186 buildings in the village are listed on the National Register of Historic Places.

(8) This from the Chamber of Commerce: "Saranac Lake is buzzing with activity in the summer. Musicians from near and afar descend on the region to perform in our parks and in our late-night venues; artists set up by Lake Flower and along our downtown strip to capture the scenery; and people with muddy hiking boots and kayaks strapped to the roof of their vehicles dart in and out of shops and restaurants. There's an energy here that can't be ignored—this is the place to be. Book a stay during our warm-weather seasons and experience our mountain village at its best!"

(9) This from the notebook of Dean Morse, aspirant author, on June 17, 1957. Rain. The rain comes on little cat's feet. Except up here this evening it feels like a big cat, a lynx or mountain lion, and at the canoe rental shop they talked about a sighting. I have heard such animals described as pumas but here they call them "catamounts." Strange name. In spite of Carl Sandburg and his "silent haunches," no fog. I'm not sure I can stomach it—not the three days of this camping trip but the whole business of teaching, the attitudes of children who are spoiled, spoiled, spoiled, spoiled, spoiled. There's a certain raw beauty of landscape, a bite in the air I might welcome if solo or, ideally, here with N. Instead I'm sitting between the two camp-provided lean-tos, hearing the boys snicker and the girls' whispered confessions: *Father, I hope to have sinned.*

They're more advanced, of course, the girls; they know much more about hormones and courtship and its rituals and who calls whom a slut. There's something touching in their attitude, which

I'm tempted to describe as a closed openness, a flower about to be plucked, what Proust called "jeunes filles en fleurs."

Though he no doubt was unpersuaded, much more taken by Albert than Albertine, and the full title of that volume is *À l'ombre des jeunes filles en fleurs.* In the shadow of their flowering, their petals soon to be clipped. Their buds pruned. All those floral metaphors: a lily, a lilac, a rose. For I seem to be the target of young Barbara the Barbie-doll or, at any rate, the one she's singled out to work her wiles on, or attempt to. She sidled up to help me spread the plastic sheet. Thank god for that, incidentally, it kept our foodstuffs dry. It will discourage the bears. Or catamounts, if catamounts there be. But practice runs and efforts at flirtation are, I'm afraid, misguided when aimed my way—those fluttered eyes, that blouse unbuttoned and those suggestive remarks:

They seek him here, they seek him there
They seek him almost everywhere . . .

I have a job to do. I have a sentence to write. The one about the trout. I have to return them, each *virgo intacta,* to the school parking lot, thence to be collected by their parents or chauffeurs and taken back to their apartments on Park Avenue or Central Park West, on Sunday evening at nine.

Mary Wollstonecraft Godwin Shelley did love her husband Percy, but he could be pompous and, because pompous, an ass. Not like his friend, the one with the club foot, who never was pompous but always an ass. "Cloven-hoofed" George was what they called him, and he was happy to dance. He did it quite badly, careening from wall to wall in the drawing room, thumping his way down and up. But he could sit a horse. And he could swim. The spectacle Lord Byron made was somehow not a clumsy one and never truly villainous or offensively suggestive, albeit one of his women accused him of being "mad, bad, and dangerous to know." Lady Caroline Lamb, the author of that intimate indictment, herself was neither sane nor good nor salubrious to consort with—being, so the rumor went, bespotted with the pox.

Mary was content, however, to know her cousin George. It was what she called him, what he wanted her to call him, "Cousin George," although they claimed no actual blood relationship, and he could make her laugh. He told a joke about scallions and leeks, which she failed to understand, but his pleasure in the telling was so manifest, infectious, that she laughed at the joke anyhow and asked him to tell it again. She was nineteen when she married Percy (although they had eloped before, when the poet was still married, his first wife not yet dead), and pleased to escape her father, William Godwin, though that widower himself had not so much escaped as remarried and withdrawn from strict parental supervision and no longer sought or required filial obedience except in its formal if insincere guise.

There were books and books and books. There were volumes in his library he urged her to consider, and others he warned would elude her, and others she would read beside her mother's grave. Alas and alack, Mary Wollstonecraft, her much-admired mother, was a person the child never knew, or barely knew: a memory of powdered cheeks, lank hair, a kiss that turned to coughing and long fingers at her neck. Even such a memory, she understood, was more a matter of invention than actual remembrance, since her mother the philosopher and feminist icon shuffled off this mortal coil when she herself was but an infant, barely one month old, and soon to be entrusted to the negligent care of their neighbor, Mary Jane Clairmont, whom in short order Godwin wed.

Quick-tempered, often quarrelsome, Mrs. Clairmont had so little of the milk of human kindness—at least in her stepdaughter's experience thereof—that the girl might just as well have suckled vinegar from the unyielding teat of some hired stranger in an airless darkened room or a monastic—nay, a prison!—cell. The prison being (like Chillon, that romantic stone pile on the island where they wandered) chill.

And therefore she had been a solitary child. She read and read and read. Her father, the great teacher, taught her little but obedience, and this she would forswear. Grand and important men— William Wordsworth, Samuel Taylor Coleridge—came to the family table, but their presence obviated hers and rendered it irrelevant to discourse over the compote or port. Her sole companions were books. Her consolation was philosophy and, in short order, romance. When the brilliant Percy Shelley professed himself her father's disciple and therefore perforce an admirer of Godwin's daughter, she was troubled by his piercing gaze and felt a flicker of excitement as he took her hand, departing, and declared it his intention—nay, spiritual certainty!—that they would meet again. Whereby hangs a tale.

But not one I plan to relate.

From the story of Prometheus, however (that Titan generous to mankind who brought them fire and consequent light), Mary took instruction, what though the man was chained to a high rock and doomed to be, forever, a meat-morsel for sharp-beaked birds assaulting his liver: this visited upon him by an angry and triumphal Zeus, who in her mind prefigured the difficult god of the Bible, that god whose name can't be pronounced for fear of retribution, and whose white hair and flowing beard were not unlike her progenitor's, who often said, "By Jove," when engaged in argument or speculation or simply surprised by a new thought or vista, for Jove is it goes without saying the Latin equivalent of the original Greek "Zeus" and perhaps the unpronounceable J——.

"The Modern Prometheus" tells a saga of bounds overstepped, of greatly daring if misplaced ambition, and that is why in 1816, the summer of their dalliance by the shores of Lake Geneva, she wrote the novel *Frankenstein* as a kind of gift to Shelley and, of course, Lord Byron, not to mention Dr. Polidori, not to mention the dogs and the monkey that cousin George maintained, as well as the peacock, the footmen, the Villa Diodati, and the dazzling vista of blue water and mountains where they took a house in Cologny.

After that encounter in her father's vestibule, she would become Percy's mistress. This, at seventeen. They eloped to France together, and when his wife, Harriet Westbrook, committed suicide, she in turn became his wife. Forever and ever, ah men. Byron too was married, to Anabella Millbanke, and they had a daughter, Ada, born in December 1815, though this did not discommode or deter him, and Mary's step-sister Claire Claremont, who was also of the party, had in England been enamored of, and—more than enamored—embroiled with them both. Both of the poets, I mean. What a lot of English names. What a lot of double-entry expenditures and complicated tallying and accounts to keep. Free love can be expensive, can it not? Free as in freely given, but what of those who take?

"A man is a man," Lord Byron wrote, "& if a girl of eighteen comes prancing to you at all hours—there is but one way."

Ah, let the wine flow copiously and the laudanum abound. Let the closed carriage and its bouncing springs, the ladies' several underthings drying on a clothesline back behind the cottage, arouse (appropriate word, well chosen!) the inquisitive if prurient interest of the citizens of Cologny. Let the nightmare vision of a mad scientist's invention be recounted to a rapt if half-drunk and dozing, nodding, audience next evening by the fire, and then write it down. Let the several body parts be by dint of unstinting labor composed into a horrific whole, and let the tale be told.

She would write other books, of course; they were a literate crew. She would become the author of such titles as *The Fortunes of Perkin Warbeck, The Last Man, Valperga,* and *History of a Six Weeks' Tour,* in which the widow narrated the story of her time in France and, thereafter, Switzerland, with the man she married and defended and promoted, what though he could be pompous and had never learned to swim. The breast-stroke, the back-stroke, the side-stroke, the crawl. Why else would he have drowned, Mary thought, how else would he—who loved to sail, who hauled the sheets as though spread beneath a coverlet and rhapsodized about the lake and sea and storm-tossed waves (the bark he was a passenger in, the orange one with splintering wood slats)—have so signally failed at the breast-stroke or back-stroke, as she herself could well attest, or just to stay afloat?

On September 16, 1822, the widow wrote: "I, the undersigned, beg the jurisdiction of Viareggio and Livorno to consign to Signore Edward Trelawney, Englishman, the boat called the *Don Juan,* and all of its contents, the property of my husband, so that it may be at his disposal." A grammatical confusion if not conflation here; who is the "his" referred to prior to "disposal," and does the writer mean to suggest that somehow her husband still lives? The contents of the wreck being books, wine bottles, a broken spyglass, and the waterlogged manuscript of his "Indian Serenade." Why consign them to Trelawney, and why was the boat called *Don Juan?*

They did die young, these poets. They were extinguished soon. Shelley's widow would live longer, and Claire Claremont would outlive them all, and write bitterly about the ways of sin, her child born out of wedlock with the cloven-footed Lord. What I'm trying to report on is the aftershock of nightmare-dreams, or wine-fueled dreams, or laudanum dreams: how Mary Wollstonecraft Godwin Shelley managed to gain and then retain the world's attention with a fable of the new Prometheus, the misbegotten marriage of intellectual ambition and science and half-mastered skill. Her monster haunts us yet.

But of whom was she a student? Of her father, of his books? Of Dr. Polidori, who—like her predecessor in marriage to Percy—committed suicide? Of the romantic man who taught her that an unacknowledged legislator might lay down the law in marriage, having slept with her half-sister early on? Of his companion who wrote of "Childe Harold" and the "Prisoner of Chillon," the one who told that joke about scallions and leeks and urged her, heartbroken, to laugh? Where, reader, in this last phrase does the apposite comma belong? Why so many questions and who, I mean, is heartbroken, the lady or man, and might it refer to them both?

Of our dozen, three remain. They too are various. As was the case in Chapter 2, the first comes to us as dialogue, the next is inward-facing and the last purports to objectivity. But each and all are variations on the theme adduced in Chapter 1, a camping trip that ends with an injunction: "Read it again."

(10) "I love you, I love you, I love you."
"How much?"
"Up to the sky and down again."
"That's an abstraction. An empty expression. How much?"
"Till a' the seas gang dry."
"Come again?"
"Through thick and thin. The whole nine yards."
"Bullshit."
"That's not being nice."
" 'Nice' comes from the Anglo-Saxon *nysse,* meaning nitwit."
"Have we just changed our diction?"
"How?"
"By shifting from the Latinate to Anglo-Saxon. The mandarin to the demotic, from high to low discourse . . ."
"Are we repeating ourself? Ourselves?"
"How? From Chapter 2?"
"By including a swearword, asshole."
"Nicely done. A pivot."
"What?"
"A pleasant little canter that. A dainty trot. *Vide* several pages previous, in the passage on Beckett and Joyce."
"I love you, I love you, I love you."

"Stop. Please stop."

"As in the doubling usage of 'Refrain?' "

"Full stop."

"Or in your letter home?"

"My first epistle, sent from Corinth?"

"The one you dictated, darling, the one where you asked me to come here in steerage and then we would be rich."

(11) Paul and Helen share a birthday; they both will turn fifteen. This knowledge of the accident of a common natal date has never mattered much before, since girls at fourteen and boys at fourteen almost belong to a separate species, and she is two inches taller, and he is only just beginning to grow hair above his lip. Not to mention balls.

But they worked together the previous month on a joint math project, using slide rules and a compass set, and the enforced proximity—her hand next to his on the twelve by twelve sheet of graph paper between them, the way she sucked her lower lip when focusing on triangles—has changed things. Altered them permanently. They have an awareness now of being somehow partnered, of sharing something with each other that the others in the bus have no real access to: July 14. For the French, he knows, their birthday is a National Holiday: Bastille Day, and everyone in France takes part in the celebration, the way Americans march in parades and set off fireworks on July 4. In eighth grade they read *A Tale of Two Cities,* and when Mme. Defarge with her knitting needles was settling the fate of those citizens of Paris who would be listed for reprisal and a bloody vengeance on the great day of the Revolution, once the Bastille was stormed and imprisoned *citoyens* set free, Paul felt—and so did Helen—that he and she were singled out.

Therefore that night by the campfire, when he'd finished with his hamburger and lukewarm coke, he let his hand rest near to hers as before it had been wont to do when they were using the slide rule and compass, grown erect when he came home, and she offered him a marshmallow so perfectly toasted—cool and damp on the inside, brown and burned at the edge—that he licked his lips afterward, tasting the remnant, the hot sweet residue, and thought about her lips. They were—he knew the expression but had never used it hitherto—"bee-stung," full and white-flecked from the marshmallow-innards she too had finished swallowing. Like cum. Which would have to wait a year, maybe two, until they were alone. In the bathroom of the Beasley apartment, when her parents were away. He standing, she on her knees.

For something premonitory passed nonetheless between them, passes between them on this wet night near the sputtering wood, the sound of a hoot owl by the lean-to where the girls will sleep, the patter of rain on the leaves of the trees, the murmuring hemlocks and pines (although anapestic trimester would urge the reverse: "the murmuring pines and the hemlocks"), that is not so much a promise as a promissory note: i.o.u. I owe you. And when the time is ripe, my love, you may collect your debt.

(12) What sort of school is this? What sort of children would take such a trip, and what are they hoping to learn? How have we come to this pass?

There are Susie, Helen, Jimmy, Paul, Dick, Richie, Evan, Barbara and me. Also, of course, Mr. Morse. Of whose future I know nothing and have not tried to learn. Neither do I propose to write about the Society of Ethical Culture, its tenets and buildings and Founding Fathers—Felix Adler and his colleagues—its reputation as a private school and budgetary allocation for scholarship and minority students and its consequential parents (from showbiz, the lit biz, the political bizness) nor the annual acceptance rate of those from Manhattan who apply (as opposed to Westchester or, *per ejemplo,* the Bronx) and the total number of applications to Fieldston Lower and then Middle School and Fieldston, its proportional success in admission of its seniors to the Ivy League, its ranking today as opposed to its ranking in the 1950s which this entry purports to describe, and the size of its endowment and annual balance sheet.

Of these ten on the camping trip, however, I do know a little, and here is the little I know. An affair of the heart will continue. It will not in fact be Helen and Paul's—though they will have the brief dalliance described, in the bathroom of her parents' apartment on March 12, 1959, an occasion he will never forget but she will not permit him to repeat, turning her attention when twenty to a same-sex affair in Smith College in her junior year, this providing her with greater pleasure and a sense of safe haven as well as reciprocity (her partner being Willa Anderson, also a junior, tall and violet-eyed and from a small town near Atlanta, majoring in French literature and writing a thesis on Gertrude Stein and Alice B. Toklas in their salon on the rue de Fleurus) thus predictive of the romantic preference she, Helen, will embrace for the mere twelve years remaining to her, since at thirty-two she will, it is my sorrowful duty to report, be hit by a white Oldsmobile '88 while entering an intersection on her bicycle, having signaled, having looked both left and right but not at the oncoming traffic, and lingering a week in pain in the Northampton Hospital—but, rather, Susie and Evan who become a "couple" in their college years and who couple more or less contentedly for the fifty-five years thereafter (with the exception of his brief affair with her step-sister Claire, and hers with a prosthetic-wearing Vietnam vet turned poet, on whom she took pity and laughed at his joke about onion and leeks), attending their Fieldston reunions, staying in touch with old classmates, living in Lexington, Massachusetts, in a split-level nine-room house with a TV Room and a Jacuzzi and a hot-tub, she a housewife, he a doctor, having two children, five grandchildren, one of whom—little Leslie Pavledes—inherits her grandmother's red hair and proclivity for freckles, until death do them part.

We are wondering, each one of us, how best to pass the night, and those of us who cannot sleep try nonetheless repeatedly to compose ourselves for sleep. Or, in the last instance, compose. These tentatives are the result: you may pack up your books. Class dismissed.

9 addenda, corrigenda

In the previous chapters—most notably in Chapter 8, but in dialogue spurts and brief scenes throughout—I deployed the techniques of prose fiction to support my argument. "Learning by doing" and "telling by showing" are time-honored strategies within the writers' trade. Close imitation may be a fruitful starting point; originality consists of starting out anew.

We are, to be precise, some 62,309 words (now 62,311, now 62,313 et seq.) into the sum and substance of that argument, and it's time to call a halt. Call it quits. What may seem, to some, a blindingly obvious assertion— with no need for repetition—may to others be a paradox that needs spelling out.

And so I will do it again. One last, one final time. My idea of a successful workshop—with, say, a dozen students—is one that produces twelve separate styles, twelve voices achieved and distinct. My idea of a failed workshop is one where each participant comes out repeating the instructor and imitating as closely as possible the style of the head of the table. It's the task of all teachers of writing to recognize and help enable an aspirant author's particular gift—her subject, his ear for dialogue, her diction, their themes. Although in Chapter 5, and elsewhere, I stress the value of ego checked at the door, it's the more important truth that what we hope to hone in workshop is each individual's talent and word choice: what sets them apart from the rest . . .

All teacher-editors know that one can turn and turn the pages of apprentice work, stifling boredom, finding nothing new, and then encounter a sentence, a paragraph, a scene that's notable. These hot spots in a narrative are hard to predict but impossible to miss; it's when an action or description or a speech or character takes wing. This is, I think, as true of verse as prose. In "Adam's Curse," the poet William Butler Yeats declares:

> A line will take us hours maybe;
> Yet if it does not seem a moment's thought,
> Our stitching and unstitching has been naught.

That word "naught" may take some discussing. It's an Anglicism, more current in England (or, in Yeats's case, Ireland) than America, where we might say "nothing" or "zero" or "zip." But after the two gerunds—"stitching and unstitching," the finality of "naught" feels apt; a monosyllabic negation undoes what went before. Imagine, further, how different the tone of the "thought" would be if the poet had written "perhaps" or "possibly" or "may-hap" or even "peradventure" instead of his preferred and collo-quial "maybe." The voice is conversational; then comes the formal "naught." It might have taken hours to come upon that closure, or the rhyming couplet ("thought" and "naught") might have come to him immediately; we readers cannot know. Which demonstrates his point.

(In fact we do have some idea, since Yeats did keep his manuscripts—though this relatively early poem has only a few drafts preserved in the Berg Collection of the New York Public Library. It comes from the 1904 volume *In the Seven Woods,* and uses a simplified diction somewhat atypical of Yeats's work at the time. It appears that "naught" was with him from the start, though other changes have been made. At first, for example, he wrote "A good line will take hours maybe," then excised the "good" and added "us" to keep the syllabic count intact. Further, it renders the assertion general; he doesn't use first-person singu-lar but the plural "us" and, two lines later, "Our." The second line began as "And yet must seem a momentary thought" before Yeats settled on the formulation "Yet if it does not seem a moment's thought," and the third line read at first, "Or all the stitching and unstichings [*sic*] naught.")

It's one of the small mysteries of the act of composition that a passage revised twenty times may look as nonchalant or casual-seeming as one that arrives whole cloth. All writers, I believe, rec-ognize that moment when words gather together unbidden, almost as though they were writing themselves and not subject to close scrutiny and hesitation and erasure. It's the difference, in effect, between vision and revision—but the final product can look, to the reader, the same. "A moment's thought," as Yeats asserts, may well be the result of hours and hours of work, but it might also be just what he claims: a moment's thought. The trick is to know when a phrase needs rephrasing, when it feels inexact or stilted or somehow misses the mark. And then to revise and revise.

So the work can be "inspired" and composed at a white heat. Or it can have been rewritten twenty times. Or it may have been rewritten twenty times. Or it may be rewritten twenty times. Or it can be composed a score of times and then scored out again. Quite often the young writer (or the old and weary one) at the end of the third or the fifth or the twelfth revision, will say, "To hell with it; this is as good as I can do." But that's a decision taken out of inattention or exhaustion or poor judgment, the automatic pilot nodding at the wheel. To "Leave well enough alone" may be a successful moral strategy; in the realm of aesthetics, however, it's a position of weakness, not strength. Excellence, it would appear, inhabits the first draft or the twenty-first; mediocrity comes between.

"Daddy, what does 'original' mean?"
"Why, Junior, what's it to you?"
"Why do you call me 'Junior' "?
"Because, kiddo, you're a chip off the old block!"
"So what does 'original' mean?"
"Indigenous, native, aboriginal, autochthonous."

"Come again?"

"Individualist, individual, eccentric, nonconformist, free
spirit, maverick."

"Daddy, why do you deny me?"

"Thrice, before cock's crow?"

"What you're saying, if I understand, is I'm not my father's
son."

"You're being derivative, Junior."

"Should I ask mother?"

"No."

There stands in front of me a carpenter's model of a bureau—
sixteen inches high and fashioned out of oak. It's early nineteenth
century, or perhaps late eighteenth century, with five small drawers and miniature metal pulls for each of them, so they slide easily
open when grasped. This piece of furniture is English, or possibly
American, and built in the "plain style." The top two rows have
two drawers each, the third and bottom row contains a single
drawer: seven inches wide. The joints are dadoed, the four feet
carved to simulate a lion's clawed feet, each at a slight angle, facing out. The whole has been stained a light brown.

Time has darkened it, so now the brown is deeper on the surface of the bureau than on the wood of the drawers' interior,
which only intermittently has been exposed to air. It might once
have served as a jewelry box, or been used as a place to store keys.
The bureau was constructed for two purposes. First, it served as
a model for the apprentice cabinetmaker who would copy it

assiduously until a full-size version might be attempted, then built. And, second, it would furnish a sample for a customer or a potential purchaser elsewhere, so the carpenter while traveling could display his wares. (In similar fashion, an itinerant luthier might carry a box of miniature violins to demonstrate his excellence; these *violons de poche* would engender a commission for a full-sized instrument built on order back at the shop.) This doubled usage—both a model and display—seems emblematic of what a successful creative writing workshop can achieve: a student works in miniature, then builds the actual thing.

❧

Young talent may burst into bloom and then fade. There are those who sicken soon (John Keats, Emily Brontë, etc.) or those turned suicidal (Sylvia Plath, John Kennedy Toole, etc.), or those killed in war (Wilfred Owen, Rupert Brooke, etc.). There are writers whose first books are their best-known titles. In our own day consider Jay McInerney's *Bright Lights, Big City* or Bret Easton Ellis's *Less Than Zero;* both authors continue to publish but to diminished acclaim. There are some whose early work is in fact their most inspired, and whose subsequent careers consist of repetition. And it's true that second novels often seem a falling-off, as if the writer has a single vein to mine. But by and large, I think, the "nature of first acts" is that there be a second act and, at full length, a third.

To return to the context of workshops, it's often if not always the case that a teacher will witness that process of growth. Ideally, the worst work one receives at the end of a semester is better than the best work one sees at the start. As the student grows more technically proficient, she or he can turn from the maker's model to a full-scale piece of furniture or—to shift the metaphor—from a half-baked to a fully seasoned dish.

This last comparison, however, is one I would urge the writer to cut, and it was composed with a view to that very excision. Let the sentence end, instead—both in the interest of clarity and efficiency—with "full-scale piece of furniture." Though even that formulation might be reconsidered, since there's no a priori evidence that bigger is better or that the intricacies of a small-scale model can be improved by enlargement. The completely achieved short story may beggar, by comparison, the loose and baggy monster that's a third-rate novel. Excellence cannot be measured by size, or size alone.

The reader will have noticed my characteristic "move." I quoted without ascription a famous phrase by Henry James, under the assumption that "loose and baggy monster" is now widely and well known. Then I put quotation marks around the word "move" so as to point it out and point it up. Further, I took a position then questioned it; made an assertion then claimed the reverse. In the previous paragraph I did so by including the phrase "a half-baked to a fully seasoned dish," then suggesting it should be excised. In the passage about "Adam's Curse" I offered three alternative versions of the original phrase, "Or it can have been rewritten twenty times."

These are, I hope, not merely self-indulgent ways of padding a page but representative of the process all authors engage in: trying a line on for size, then deciding if it works. *Variora:* Trying on a line for size and deciding if it works. Trying on a line for size, then seeing if it works. Trying on a line for size to see if it will fit. Trying on a line for size. Trying on a phrase as though it were a line of clothing and seeing if it "suits." Trying on a line as though it were a piece of clothing and seeing if it suits. Standing in front of a mirror, examining the sleeve and seeing (as though it were a sentence) how it fits. Standing on a tailor's platform, examining yourself in the three-sided full-length wood-framed mirror while the new assistant tailor—that lissome girl from Romania, recently arrived to work in her uncle's establishment, a needle in her thin white hand and white thread dangling from her mouth—kneels at your feet and embraces your ankle and asks if this is the length you prefer, the width of cuff you desire, her words engagingly muffled not merely by the difficulties of new-acquired English but also the white thread dangling wetly from her pink and half-closed and, for so slight a woman, surprisingly full lips, long lashes fluttering, eyes blue, and is it possible she has a lisp even in her native tongue, or is her question as to length while she encircles your right foot somehow suggestive, intimate? (her uncle at the store's far rear, bent over an ironing board and therefore unable to provide his customary close and even jealous supervision of her apprentice labor but, rather, unaware of or at any rate too far removed to monitor the transaction in progress up front near the changing room). Let me now more accurately describe it: the space is not so much a changing room as four-by-four square cubicle, its curtain fluttering in the fan-engendered breeze, its eight by twelve inch mirror nailed to the white sheetrock wall, a shelf for shoes and scarves and shirts and skirts, a bare bulb with a frayed chord dangling from the socket, a photograph of mountains and a photograph of goats, its privacy on offer for a rapid assignation where your pants already hang—the pants you wore on entry and doffed to don this soon-to-be altered and just-purchased pair (her fingers at your ankle, her head bent down, approaching it submissively on this hot September 24 at 3:37 p.m.). How old are you, you want to ask—nineteen, twenty-one, twenty-three?—and how long my dear have you been in this country and do you like it here and do you plan to stay? while, in seeming-negligence but in fact with carefully contrived intention, and as you grow tumescent which she cannot fail to notice, since her mouth with its white thread dangling spittle-like, half-open, moist, is now positioned at the level of your serge-swathed crotch, and while she glances shyly—shyly, or is it slyly?—up in response at where you balance bulging on the wooden platform and the momentary pedestal from which you must descend you ask yourself, and cannot help but wonder if this very escapade has been rehearsed and earlier enacted—how often, with how many men?—so that the background music now emerging from the static-raddled radio by the cash register is not a song of innocence but experience, and she whom you believed at first to be free from worldly knowingness (a large part of her charm and erotic allure) is in fact available for purchase as a by-blow of the tailoring. "Why then, Ile fit you," or did she with that muffled lisp and inflected accent mean to say "Why then, I'll sit you, mad Hieronymo?"—and must you therefore revise your opinion as to that distant uncle; did he in fact engineer and does he approve of and will he require a percentage of the profit from the encounter soon to follow in the changing cubicle, the space itself transformed by her nubile nakedness, spread-eagled on the white pine shelf and urging you, the customer, to enter, while in this equivocal moment you let your left hand rest on her shoulder as though for balance and stability, but in fact pressing and assessing the sharp clavicle like fruit.

Block that metaphor. Cut "the sharp clavicle like fruit."

"You must obey me."

"Master, I will obey you."

"Good."

"Master, how may we proceed?"

"Dust off the synecdoche. Polish the cliché until it shines anew. Revive the palindrome. Let it gleam."

".maelg ti teL .emordnilap eht eviveR"

"Able was I ere I saw Elba. Madam, I'm Adam. A man, a plan, a canal: Panama!"

"Oh, *that's* how you do it."

"We do it."

"Agreed."

"Tell me, was the echo intentional? The perfect rhyme with, eight lines ago, "proceed"?"

"It was, sir, yes."

"And the reference some lines back to Blake, his songs of *Innocence* and *Experience*. That too?"

"Those too."

"Was the cuff a penile cuff? At least by adjacency?"

"Yes."

"And when you wrote, or at any rate alluded to, *Hieronymo's mad againe,* were you referencing *The Waste Land*? Or *The Spanish Tragedy*?

"This grows tedious, Master. The twain."

Several other aspects of the workshop experience and culture may be worth discussing. It's almost unavoidable that the apprentice author should have career concerns. In our celebrity moment, and with paychecks on the line, it can be difficult to honor anonymity or writing done for free. At some point in all authors' lives, the matter of success arises, and questions do get asked. "Is the work good enough, is it publishable, will it be published, how do I find an agent, an editor, a job?"

An MFA in Writing degree is something very different than, say, a graduate degree in business or medicine or law. In these latter instances, the verdict is delivered more or less concomitant with the diploma; if you don't have a job with a law firm or clinic or consulting company once you've been credentialed, you're in trouble—or anyhow non-representative. The shape of a career in those several disciplines can be predicted and to a degree established early on. You graduate at the top of your class or in the lower quadrant; you're offered employment by a white-shoe law firm or the guy with a sign in the window above a shuttered store on Main Street, whose last assistant decamped in July; your starting salary is in six figures, or on commission, or minimum wage . . .

A writer, however, may take five or fifteen years to demonstrate accomplishment and then to enter "the guild." There's no guarantee of employment once a novel or a book of short stories or poems has been finished, even published, and the very popularity of writing programs—scarce as hens' teeth once—makes the recent graduate less likely to find work. Over the past several decades the study of creative writing has proved a growth industry; in part because of this there are more graduates each year who "profess" it than there are slots to fill. At entry level in the academy (still a preferred destination for those with MFA degrees), supply exceeds demand.

The teacher may well feel that A or B or C has the most talent in a room, but D and E are the ones who emerge with book contracts instead. Contests proliferate; small magazines earn a large part of their annual budget from entry fees for juried awards that promise publication, and everywhere, to quote Yeats again, "the ceremony of innocence is drowned."

Since the process of admission to a writing program is selective—highly so in the highly ranked ones—the idea of competition is intrinsic to the enterprise; it's not "first-come first-serve" as a system but one that begins with a test. Often, those tests and contests continue: who gets a full scholarship plus stipend, who gets a teaching assistantship, who gets a grader's subsidy, who has to pay full freight to enroll? and so on down the line. Competitive feelings are hard to dismiss, and one might even argue that—in the cut-throat business of professional achievement, prize winning, and networking—the skill of self-promotion is a skill to cultivate. Which is why an author, now, must have a Facebook or Twitter account, a blog or personal platform in order to increase a book's potential audience; the article or book or poem must not only be written but sold . . .

At the more prestigious writing programs (the ones at Columbia, Iowa, Michigan, the University of Texas at Austin, for example), agents visit and sign up young hopefuls, since the raw material of the publishing industry—language—is in those institutions produced. To discover and promote young talent is part of the agents' trade. For the apprentice, therefore, to go "where the action is" is a strong temptation, and rankings attach to such programs, as they do to those in medicine and law. Students jockey for position and the chance to be—in some cases, alas, literally—"teacher's pet." The writer and editor Ted Solotaroff used to argue that the proper subject of a writing workshop should be "How to Deal with Rejection," since rejection is the artist's common lot. Remember good King Arthur and his round table; those knights who were not seated near the king might well complain they sat "below the salt" . . .

But that's precisely why a workshop should be set apart. There's world enough and time, I think, for aspiring writers to deal with the professional world. My own strong preference, in class, was and is to ignore or set aside all such considerations and focus on the prose. The years dedicated to the acquisition of an MFA degree are, or should be, separate from those that come before and after.

All this for reasons that may take some spelling out.

First, at any writing program worth entering there will be subsidies and, ideally, the student can earn a diploma for free. If you study—to use, again, our previous examples—business or medicine or law, you graduate with a realistic expectation that your debt can be discharged, and you'll earn steady income in the years ahead. But for the recipient of a Master of Fine Arts degree (whether in creative writing or music or the visual arts), that fiscal expectation is at best a gambler's guess. To emerge from such a course of study with tens of thousands of dollars in debt is to be indentured for more than the seven years of traditional apprenticeship, and it's too often the case.

From the start of my time in Ann Arbor, as director of the MFA Program in Writing at the University of Michigan, I worked to change those odds. It seemed and seems to me that those who choose the writers' trade should not be disadvantaged by debt, or required to do hack work to pay off what they owe. Therefore much of my time at Michigan was spent in fund-raising to reach the goal of full fiscal support, and—thanks to a munificent gift by Helen Herzog Zell—our goal has been achieved. Enabled by the Zell family foundation, it's now the rule that no one admitted to what has been properly renamed the Helen Zell Writers' Program will graduate with a penny of debt, and this after three years. So the period of study can be burden-free and focused in a way that sets it apart from the workaday world and the career trajectory to come.

Second, the life of the professional author is in central ways a lonely one. I don't mean to cry crocodile tears on the writer's behalf, but the work is done in isolation and almost always without immediate response. Even if a book gets published, it's likely to take a good while to appear, and by then the writer—if he or she be scrupulous—is engaged on and by another project. There's no reaction—whether great praise, great dispraise, or (the most likely) a benign neglect—that's anything other than a gravitational side-drag upon the forward motion of the work at hand. To receive a fan letter or a good review is of course a welcome thing but almost always irrelevant to the labor of writing itself.

I mean by this that the point and counterpoint that we take to be the norm of human interaction is denied the writer. Communication—as good a term as any for what most authors try to achieve—is a two-way street. Every act of artistic creation is a dialogue, not monologue; each stimulus provokes, or should, a measurable response. An actor or musician will know, almost on the instant, how the audience feels about their performance; an athlete knows at the close of a race or game if it's been won or lost. Yet a writer requires months and maybe years to earn a positive or negative reaction. Nor is it often germane. The fan who writes a letter will tell you her Aunt Sadie also went to Machu Picchu once; the critic who complains that your stallion is a gelding will be riding his own hobby-horse; the friend who feels compelled to praise your work will have read it rapidly, and out of duty rather than desire. The dedicated reader is a *rara avis* indeed . . .

In a writing workshop, however, this is not the case. In our imagined group of twelve, when your work comes under scrutiny, you have eleven witnesses who pay close attention and offer up their thoughts. If only because these fellow participants hope to have, when their turn comes, an attentive reading, they will provide one for you, and hard on the heels of creation. There's risk attached to this; most original work takes time to gestate fully, and too many contradictory suggestions may create confusion. Some young writers cringe at critiques and prefer to work in privacy. But it's almost always useful to be told, while engaged in a project, that this is a path to follow and that a line to cut. If you trust your colleagues (and no workshop can succeed without at least a component of trust), you leave the session with advice that helps you power forward through the draft. This too is a comparative rarity and will not be repeated in the "professional" years.

Third, and finally, we all are selective as readers. We know on the instant, paging through a magazine or newspaper, if we want to read an article; we know rapidly, when standing in a bookstore or in front of a library shelf, which book to pick and take home. There's no contractual expectation, further, that we must finish what we start; as an editor once told me, when talking of the "slush pile," "I'm always looking for a chance to stop reading." The first line or first page or first chapter may be sufficient to tell us we don't need to continue; quite often the experience of reading is a distracted one, and attention wanders until we close the book.

But in a writing workshop that's very rarely true. Again, if only because all students hope their own work will be carefully attended to, they're honor-bound to scrutinize the work of others at the table. You read all the way to the end of the story or chapter under discussion, even if it disappoints you, and formulate a response. In a culture where the skills of composition are largely taken for granted or devalued, it's inspiriting to share a space with those who share your belief in the craft and practice it together. That lonely life referred to earlier gets put on hold.

All this is, it may be, an unspoken or even unconscious agreement: the rules of the game each member of a workshop plays during the MFA years. But it will not happen again. To have a tight-knit group of colleagues give close consideration to your work is a luxury few practitioners have, and one they mourn when it's gone. (It's part of the reason that "writers' groups" or "readers' circles" have proliferated lately; many graduates of MFA programs try to keep their old circle unbroken, and to stay in touch.) But it's why I'm always moved, at semester's start, by the gathering of apprentice authors at a table. They once were total strangers; soon, they'll know each other well. Their work once had only one reader; soon it will be shared. Earlier they labored in "silence, exile, and cunning"; soon, they will have colleagues in the craft.

I don't mean to overstate this, but there's something quasi-sacred about the chance to devote oneself, wholly and uninterruptedly, to the creation of a work of art. And to do so in a company whose values are the same. I reverence this opportunity and try to impart that sense of reverence to others in the room.

"Let's have a talk."
"All right."
"A conversation."
"All *right!*"
"A proper bit of dialogue."
"You got it, bro."
"A Socratic dialogue."

"Mistah Socrates, he dead."

"Don't go getting cute with me."

"The farthest thing from my intention, sir."

"So what do we talk about?"

"You pick the topic. I respond."

"Call and response?"

"You could call it that. Why not?"

"Stichomythia?"

"Because the single line of dialogue, in regular alternation
and exchange, can grow wearisome."

"You can say that again."

"Because the single line of dialogue, in regular alternation
and exchange, can grow wearisome."

"Too true."

Another aspect of the trade is worth considering. The study and teaching of writing, which has been a focus of this book, is neither time-bound nor transient. It's not as though the making of a phrase or scene can be a puzzle that, once puzzled out, gets permanently solved. To repeat a sentence (as I've just done in the dialogue above) is not to repeat a solution, since the problems change. Neither tic-tac-toe nor the Rubik's Cube describes the challenge of a paragraph; there's no one way to build it, no single right answer or way to proceed.

Rather, each time we start again we start out afresh. I'm no expert at liposuction or real-estate law, but I imagine that the skills of surgery and litigation can—after years and decades—

start to feel repetitive; once you've mastered such procedures you hope *not* to be surprised. The difficulty confronting you will be at worst a subset of a long-familiar whole. But surprise is the writer's constant companion; without it, the work languishes and gets performed by rote. Each sentence is a riddle; each paragraph a test. So more than fifty years after my first book-length publication, I'm still in some sense a beginner, and every morning's challenge is to begin anew. I'm aware of my ability to bring a book to completion, and not fearful of the daily task, but no more certain now than then that what I'm working on will gain other people's attention, or deserve to.

There are formulaic writers who provide themselves a template and, with a greater or lesser degree of success, continue and repeat. Such formulae resemble the procedures of a "paint by numbers" program, or instruct you to "Fill in the blanks." Yet the creative artist never fully knows, at a project's start, if it will reach fruition—or if the shape at first envisioned will be its final shape. And even if you come to feel that what you've done is perfect, or as close to perfection as you can come, there's the certain knowledge that some flaw is hidden, or disguised; a pattern in the carpet where the stitching shows.

And unstichings (*sic*) come to naught.

In this sense the "sense of an ending"—whether it be a work of literary criticism by Frank Kermode (1967), a novel by Julian Barnes (2011), or a critical inquiry into late style by Edward Said, Helen Vendler, et al.—is incomplete, and necessarily so. No matter how high the gloss and bright the polish of a work of art, it's unfinished and provisional. So when I wrote, at chapter's start, that "Excellence, I think, inhabits the first draft or the twenty-first," I did not mean to dismiss the possibility of a twenty-second or twenty-third; there's always more to be done.

"In conclusion," therefore—that welcome moment when a speaker signals that a speech draws near to closure—I want to assert that there's no real conclusion. A hiatus, yes, pause certainly, a drawing in of breath and grateful exhalation, but not the end of learning how to shape a book. Which is, or should be, a lifelong process, a procedure begun in childhood and continued from cradle to grave. The writer who believes there's nothing left to learn is one who should lay down his pen or turn off her computer; the one who claims full mastery is lodging a false claim. What Keats called "negative capability"—the willingness to take a position not a priori one's own—is crucial to the craft. My hope in this discussion is to have raised questions rather more than given answers, because the questioning intelligence is one that can embrace the possibility of change.

Where once the landscape of American letters was, by common agreement, a plain from which three mountains rose—William Faulkner, F. Scott Fitzgerald, and Ernest Hemingway—the view has altered now. In a long-overdue correction, the world of writers and readers has grown much more inclusive and various. Contemporary literature comes a good deal closer to mirroring our nation's population and its domestic as well as public concerns; the "dead white men" who once dominated the culture are merely a component part of the collective whole.

Our great late Nobel laureate in literature from the United States, Toni Morrison, has paved the way for countless other authors who had been marginalized a generation previous. (Bob Dylan, our more recent laureate, also breaks new ground.) The careers of such "women of color" as Sandra Cisneros, Jamaica Kincaid, and Jhumpa Lahiri have been at least in part enabled by the careers of Maxine Hong Kingston and Alice Walker, who "walked the walk" before. All indices in the publishing industry—the number of titles, the size of their sales, the prizes earned and honors accrued—attest to this: "minority" literature is no longer a useful description or an operative term.

In Chapter 5 I celebrated the work of Jesmyn Ward, and how her career took wing. Let me name, at near random, a dozen additional graduates from the program in prose fiction in Ann Arbor. Uwem Akpan, Brittany Bennett, Randa Jarrar, Akil Kumarasamy, Rattawut Lapcharoensap, Lilian Li, Nami Mun, Celeste Ng, Chigozie Obioma, Preeta Samarasan, Inez Tan, and Esmé Wang have each published collections of short stories or novels that earned respectful attention—and, in the case of Mr. Akpan and Ms. Ng, attained best-seller status. Many other writing programs can claim much the same, for there's been a true expansion—even an explosion—of the voices of immigrant authors, young artists of differing skin tints and sexual preferences and gender self-identifications and social strata and creeds. It's something of which we can be justly proud and signals major change.

A corollary here. It's not news that literary reputations rise and fall, or that death is the great leveler. Of the three "masters" I discussed in Chapter 1, I think it fair to say that John Updike's reputation has declined to one of respected irrelevance; far fewer read him today. John Gardner, once so present on the scene, is almost wholly absent now, and knowledge of his novels or, say, his *On Moral Fiction* (1978) seems rare. This may well change, of course, and Fortune's wheel revolve once more. For it has done so with a vengeance in the case of the third, James Baldwin, whose reputation soars and whose sales increase. One—admittedly small—aspect of that increase is the movie *I Am Not Your Negro* in 2017, which brought the writer's voice and face indelibly forward to a new generation of readers and reminded those who read him before that they should do so again. This holds true, as well, for the major release in 2018 of Barry Jenkins's movie version of *If Beale Street Could Talk* (1974). What brings Baldwin back to prominence is not only the page but the screen.

More importantly, no doubt, a principal subject of his prose—the sorry state of race relations in America—has not gone away. The world of Harry Angstrom, the protagonist of Updike's "Rabbit" tetralogy, looks more and more like an act of retrieval: an elegant description of behavior in the past. And Gardner's *personae* and story lines feel more than a little arcane. But Baldwin's characters and their concerns are just as alive now as then. His essays and plays and book-length nonfictions and novels and a children's book are at one and the same time prophetic and current; his searing rhetoric and personal imperatives stay pertinent today.

The Association of Writers and Writing Programs (AWP) was established forty years ago. At the most recent annual conference—by far the largest literary event in North America, and one that moves from city to city—there were twelve thousand attendees. In 2018 there were two thousand presenters; 550 panel discussions and readings took place; more than eight hundred presses, journals, and literary magazines went on display at the "in house" book fair. The once-small group of renegades and outliers from the MLA (Modern Language Association) has, as an institution, prospered mightily. The AWP is now a behemoth and one that continues to grow.

Degree-conferring graduate programs, whether full- or low-residency, are equally in the growth mode; though they once numbered fewer than a dozen, there are several hundred today. You can't throw a rock in New England without hitting a writer's conference, and the credential of an MFA has become a near necessity for those who wish to study writing and, when the time comes, to teach. This is all the more remarkable because, in the curriculum, close study of English is at risk; enrollment has fallen precipitously in the liberal arts in general and literature in particular. Yet from coast to coast throughout the nation, writing programs spring up hydra-headed, with no outer limit in sight. How best to explain this seeming paradox: the legion of young aspirant authors, most of them ready to go into debt, who hope to join the swelling tide of those who, more than likely, will fail at or fail to prosper in the writers' trade?

A part of this, perhaps, has to do with the rags-to-riches component of the American dream. It's not confined to writers but true as well for those who dream of prominence in, say, entertainment or athletics; almost by definition, we learn only the stories of those who succeed and not of those who don't. For every sweet-voiced singer who makes it to the top of the charts, there are hundreds, maybe thousands, who rarely or never get heard. For every football player with a multi-million-dollar contract, there are hundreds, maybe thousands, with damaged bodies and minds. But on magazine covers and television talk shows we see and hear the ones who've come out of nowhere into prominence and therefore tell ourselves that our turn too may come. It's what powers the purchase of lottery tickets or avid crowds in casinos: the Holy Grail of wealth and fame that all gamblers hope they may someday attain.

As long ago as the reign of Queen Elizabeth I (1558–1603) this dynamic was in place. The canny queen played favorites. She knew she couldn't afford to keep her English nobles in the style to which they thought they ought to be accustomed, and knew as well she needed them at court, not in the countryside where they might foment insurrection. So every year or three she'd honor someone out of proportion to actual merit; she'd say to Walter Raleigh, for instance, "You put your cloak in a puddle so my own feet wouldn't get muddy; I thank you and grant you Virginia!"

Then all the other nobles would elbow each other and say, "We're just as good as Raleigh; let's sell the castle in Scotland and wait here another season when the Queen will surely notice us instead. Our time will come!"

I'm being reductive, of course, but the court of Queen Elizabeth does seem a kind of model for the literary life. The sight of some sudden "favorite" who signs a large contract or sells to the movies keeps many young writers at work, imagining their own next page or project will take wing. If it happens to X, thinks Y, why can't it happen to me?

Art traffics in the unexpected, and there's no sure or single path to success. Every month some new voice emerges and is widely praised; each year some new writer gains fame. And this dream of possibility beguiles us all, though statistical odds are long. As W. H. Auden put it pithily, in his *Squares and Oblongs:*

> The ideal audience the poet imagines consists of the beautiful who go to bed with him, the powerful who invite him to dinner and tell him secrets of state, and his fellow-poets. The actual audience he gets consists of myopic schoolteachers, pimply young men who eat in cafeterias, and his fellow-poets. This means that, in fact, he writes for his fellow-poets.

But that's a worthy and not negligible audience, and the rewards are intrinsic as well as extrinsic for any aspirant author. So write they do and write we will, and more and more are doing so each day. It's what keeps us at the desk.

❧

"Is this correct?"

"The length, you mean?"

"Yes. Length."

"I like it that way, yes."

"And the cuff? You wish a cuff?"

"Indeed."

"Just so?"

"Just so."

"Stand more straighter, please Mister."

"I'm sorry."

"Not a problem."

"Excuse me?"

"It's what you say in this country, I think."

"Oh, yes. No problem."

"My English is not good, I think."

"It's better than my Romanian."

"Ha. You make a joke?"

"I meant it to be funny, yes."

"You're very kind."

"And how is your uncle to work for?"

"Not so always very kind."

"Let's fuck."

This last suggestion is, perhaps, not wholly unexpected—given the imagined scene spun out some pages ago. But it should, I hope, have come with a small shock of recognition, a sense that something other than politeness is at play in the conversation between customer and tailor just rendered, with more than one thing happening at once. It shifts the diction too. I meant to suggest her syntax and grasp of English are uncertain; he uses time-worn Anglo-Saxon monosyllables with his two-word proposition at exchange's end. What her response will be is open to question, a pause . . .

Whether my imagined Romanian tailor is submissive or suggestive is, I hope, impossible to tell with any certainty from the dialogue as such. Nor can we tell with any certainty if the

"Mister" speaking here is moved by her predicament or taking advantage thereof. Is the author being funny; is he being serious; did he once overhear or himself engage in this conversation or make it entirely up?

All fictions worth writing or reading rely on the conveyed impression that, as in life, there are depths. A conversation or action may be reported on from several vantage points, and what A concludes might well stand separate from the conclusions of B or C. Ford Madox Ford called this lack of clarity (and consequent multiplicity) "Impressionism." It organized his narrative procedure, the advance by indirection and digression that was his chosen mode. He believed—along with Joseph Conrad, with whom he for a time collaborated—that the high task of literature "is . . . to make you see." That quotation comes from Conrad's "Preface to 'The Nigger of the Narcissus' " (1897), and it's the central tenet of their shared aesthetic. (The N-word, it need scarcely be noted, has a different connotation and tonal import now than then.) Impressionism, in the verbal not visual arts, is meant to mimic and thereby convey the complexity of sensory alertness; we see more than one thing at one time. We hear no single note but a chord.

Virginia Woolf felt much the same way and, in "Modern Fiction" (arguing against the conventional novels of Bennett, Galsworthy, Wells, et al.), wrote:

> Look within, and life, it seems, is very far from being "like this."
> Examine for a moment an ordinary mind on an ordinary day. The
> mind receives a myriad impressions—trivial, fantastic, evanescent,
> or engraved with the sharpness of steel . . . Life is not a series of
> gig lamps symmetrically arranged; life is a luminous halo, a

semi-transparent envelope surrounding us from the beginning of consciousness to the end.

Ford, Conrad, and Woolf have in common the desire to explain themselves—to describe the purpose of their own and particular prose styles. An artist is, more often than not, the best apologist for his or her aesthetic; it helps in the reading of Sir Philip Sydney, for example, to read his *Defense of Poesie* (1580), or John Dryden, a hundred years later, with his *Essay of Dramatick Poesie* (1688). William Wordsworth, Samuel Taylor Coleridge, T. S. Eliot, Audre Lorde, Adrienne Rich, and many other poets provide in their criticism a kind of roadmap to their own terrain; explanation if not self-justification is part of the writer's trade.

In some sense I could argue that this chapter and book are just such an effort, and my model of apprenticeship seems self-reflexive, clearly. It's inescapably the case that one's personal experience enlarges into generality, and when I wrote to start with of my gratitude to teachers, I was paying off a long-term debt via this small installment. Those writers I paid homage to (Updike, Gardner, Baldwin) and those who taught me early on (Morse, Lenrow, Alfred, Morrison), each had, in turn, their own instructors, and though time and the river have done their slow work, the lesson plans and lessons learned endure. For every "original" author there's a long origin story, and even if the influence be only dimly perceived or unacknowledged, there's influence involved.

On August 1, 1899, Sigmund Freud wrote, in a letter to Wilhelm Fleiss, "And I am accustoming myself to the idea of regarding every sexual act as a process in which four persons are involved." It's my contention that the same holds true of language; each line has antecedents, and every tale a shadow-companion. There are precedents and prior usage everywhere. We come from what went before.

"Ego te absolvo."

"Of?"

"Excessive quotation."

"And why?"

"Because it is the stuff of learned experience. In literature.
    The liner for the pantry shelf whereon to store our stock."

"Our stock in trade."

"And is this not delightful? And does it not delight?"

"Not really, no."

"The oxymoron. Periphrasis. Catachresis in the watches of the night."

"Now *you're* the one who's using rhyme."

"Iamb."

"And an atrocious pun."

"That too."

"This can't go on."

"All right."

I began this book in praise of books by Sylvia Ashton Warner and Eudora Welty. In *Teacher* and *One Writer's Beginnings,* "The first person enters in, as it must in any autobiographical account, but in neither instance does the writer insist on stage center." For this final entry I confess the first-person pronoun entered here rather more than first intended, and a consideration of the importance of writing became as well an *Apologia Pro Vita Sua*. What was conceived of, early on, as an account of *Why Writing Matters* became an essay on the things I learned and taught.

As suggested earlier, this may be unavoidable and might indeed have been my subject from the start. I discovered and uncovered it as I went along. But if the previous chapters have been, at times, personal or playful, I want to close with the great last couplet of the great English playwright's last play. The magician Prospero provides an exit line for every author since *The Tempest*. When he comes out on stage alone to ask for and receive applause, he says,

> As you from crimes would pardon'd be
> Let your indulgence set me free . . .

No clearer closure than this; no lines with more resounding finality. Yet one can wonder nonetheless which freedom the magician and his creator aspired to: what it meant to be "set . . . free." Does the speaker wish to return to an imagined Naples or Milan, or—in Shakespeare's case—the actual Stratford-on-Avon? Does he plan to go backstage and "retire" to the Tiring House (that small structure back behind the Globe) in order to change costume and go out on the town for a drink; does he ask for "your indulgence" with a wink and nod or true humility?

Much of the speech contains religious imagery ("And my ending is despair / Unless I be relieved by prayer / Which pierces so that it assaults / Mercy itself and frees all faults"), but does the playwright here declare a formal faith? Will Prospero start a new career, or resume his old honored position as duke? The "revels now are ended," yes, but is it necessarily the case that "Every third thought shall be my grave"? Did he truly mean, as at the close of *Hamlet,* that "The rest is silence"? There's the sense of completion, and a request for approval, but are the terms of the simile correct and does the comparison hold: has the previous play been a crime?

Early on in *The Tempest,* the man-beast Caliban—an anagram for Can(n)ibal—tells Prospero: "You taught me language, and my profit on't / Is I know how to curse. The red plague rid you / For learning me your language!" (act 1, scene 2). This too is pronounced, I'd guess, in the ironic mode, because that curse had been a blessing for the bard. No one has ever written with a greater range of discourse or engendered more delight in it; no writer instructed us more. It's fitting he appeared with greater frequency than any other author in these pages; we are his students, all. What he taught himself more than four hundred years ago is what we continue to learn.

Yet one need not imitate Shakespeare (who is, in any case, inimitable) to assert that such direct address—the actor in front of an audience, standing stage center and confronting his patrons directly—is the proper way to close. "This rough magic I here abjure," he had promised earlier, in the renunciation scene where Prospero gives up his spells and drowns his book. Great thanks it was recovered, preserved, and passed on.

postscript

What does it mean to have language "passed on," and what by such retention has been "recovered, preserved"? Had no one written down the final words of Shakespeare's Prospero—in a prompt book, then a folio—we would not quote them now. Although there still are cultures with extensive oral history, the way one generation learns and profits from its predecessors comes more and more routinely through the medium of print. A transmission of what went before depends on this matter of writing, and those cultures with no written record stand at risk. But the nature of what's written down is also consequential, and the stewards of a language are honor-bound to monitor its use.

I mean by this that those of us who spend our lives in the service of English should guard against debasement—the lies and half-truths and propaganda deployed so routinely today. A machinist cannot be approximate when measuring the size of a screw or fabricating a nut and bolt; a musician can't play sharp or flat and hope to stay in tune. A surgeon needs to know exactly which bone or artery must be repaired, and how to effect the repair. In every profession I know of, there is theory to acquire and practical usage to hone.

But because we've been using our language since we first began to speak, read, write, we tell ourselves the mechanics of English are skills we need not attend to—much the way we fail to notice how we walk or breathe. And too often for too many writing *doesn't* matter; it's a skill to ignore or dismiss. As I wrote in Chapter 5, it's the kind of familiarity with established usage that can breed contempt. If some catastrophic accident or illness forces us to pay attention—to learn, as adults, how to walk or breathe again—we may renew appreciation for what we took for granted, then study movement closely till we master it once more. But by and large the native practitioner of English takes only casual notice of what was learned when young. All too often there's regression and all too rarely advance.

In *The Nation's Report Card,* which describes itself as "the largest ongoing assessment of what U.S. students know and can do," there's a disconcerting graph: 28 percent of matriculated students read at the fourth-grade level, 27 percent at the eighth-grade level, and only 27 percent are proficient at or above the level of twelfth grade. In the *National Assessment of Adult Literacy* (conducted by the U.S. Department of Education), the results are much the same; 14 percent of the adults surveyed are below the basic literacy level and only 13 percent are proficient. For a nation founded on the ideals of democracy, in which an educated populace determines its own future, this is grim news indeed. If you choose to read this book, and can absorb its argument, you're the exception to the rule of those entitled to vote. And whatever your political leanings, the lack of widespread competence in the skills of language is a condition to mourn.

Although some literary prodigies have an almost preternatural-seeming "gift of tongues" (think of Crane, Keats, or Rimbaud), there's no such thing as an author who does his or her best work in childhood; it's an acquired skill. Those habits we formed in the nursery or schoolyard may often be bad habits, or at least improved by study—the way an actress will practice elocution or an actor learn an accent not native to his speech. All performers understand the need for repeated rehearsal; that writing too is a performance should not come as news.

The title of this brief last section, "Postscript," means, in its original usage, "after the thing written." By convention it's the opposite of "Preface," or, "before the thing that's made." (The terms derive from Latin; their Greek equivalents are *prologue* and *epilogue*—"before and after the word.") However we choose to label it, a final entry should serve both as a new departure and a summing up.

There are more than seven billion members of the species *Homo sapiens* at present on our planet, and at a rough guess only a third of us possess the skills of composition; it's not something we are born with, like the gift of locomotion or breath. Many live this life without a pen or page. In the roster of survival skills, literacy ranks low. Yet those who cannot write or read are burdened by the deficit; it's a barrier and line of demarcation most sentient beings aspire to cross. To repeat a claim of this book's Preface, "it's imagination linked to knowledge and a central mode of growth."

Throughout this text, it's been my contention that the mastery of written discourse is neither instinctual nor automatic. It takes time to learn. Clear expressiveness and proper grammatical usage may not be ends in and of themselves, but they are nonetheless part of the means by which a line is "justified." The now-out-moded practice of copying something down on blackboards ten or twenty or a hundred times did teach the recalcitrant student how letters and words shape a phrase. If nothing else, we learned by rote the distinction between lowercase and uppercase letters, and how to form them precisely. Without the skills of composition, we grow thick-fingered, tongue-tied, mute.

Note, please, in these last two sentences how the mode of discourse shifts from writing to speech: how closely they are linked. The one implies the other; the former requires the latter. As Alberto Manguel, in *A History of Reading,* observes: "All writing depends on the generosity of the reader." The reverse is also true. The two methods of communication profit from each other in a kind of symbiosis, and only the exceptional individual—by which I mean the one who proves the rule—uses language in its written or its spoken form alone.

Such homonyms as "write" or "right" or "wright" each have a separate meaning, and there's a further distinction between homograph and homophone (the orthography or pronunciation of similar-sounding words). "Polish" and "polish" use the same spelling but have very separate connotations; "pole" and "poll" have different meanings but echo each other in speech. "Wont" and "won't" are pronounced and mean things unalike; why should a punctuation mark make such a difference? The three words "to" and "too" and "two" sound the same but represent distinct and unrelated entities; in each instance, context is all.

This is why, perhaps, a fluency in English is so hard to come by for non-native speakers; such arrangements of diction and inflection are not self-evident. Why should "taught" and "taut" mean different things, and why are the "g" and "h" silent? Three paragraphs ago I put quotation marks around the one word "justified." The term has two principal meanings. In the abstract sense it has to do with justice and the defense of a position; in the concrete sense it means the way the margins of a page will be aligned. Why?

Let us imagine, in writing, how a world without writing might function. This is a self-negating proposition, clearly, and one that can't be addressed by means of and in the context of writing itself. But, for a moment, let's try. What would it mean if nothing were written, if the pronouncement "I give you my word" were sufficient as a contract, and if laws and liabilities were not codified as letters and words on a page? All language would be spoken text, except that "text" would not exist and what we'd as a species rely on would be only, entirely, speech. The great preserved works of our culture would have been doomed to extinction, the records we keep null and void. Had I written "void and null," at least a few readers would question the reversal of terms in the formulaic phrase, but without a readership (because there is no writing)

there would have been no eyebrow raised or effort at correction; had I written "zoid" and "gull" it would have made no difference, since neither a robot nor seabird would have been by those letters described.

We operate, I mean, under the assumption that language is in crucial part a written thing, and not merely spoken or signed. Our culture is so indebted to and organized by writing that it's difficult to reconstruct a place and time where it failed to signify, and mankind did without. The system of transmitted knowledge requires a visual as well as verbal exchange of information; what we fail to remember we read. And even those whose memory is encyclopedic will have an outer limit to what can be recalled.

For a professional pleb of words it's doubly difficult, somehow, to imagine a world without writing, but all of us who take written language for granted would be, I think, shocked by its disappearance and in its absence aggrieved. It's the *alpha* and *omega,* the *a* to *z* of what we learn from predecessors, the Rosetta Stone of culture even when those cultures have long been extinct.

When the Rosetta Stone itself—a granodiorite stele found by French soldiers in the Egyptian desert in 1799—was brought back to Europe and finally deciphered, we learned much. The decree had been recorded in three languages and inscribed in 196 BCE in the reign of King Ptolemy V. It proclaimed the king's divinity and the excellent accomplishments of his so-far reign; it was intended to be understood by all of the king's subjects and therefore was composed in three modes.

The first of these was hieroglyphic and (to the eighteenth-century reader) entirely opaque; the second was demotic Greek, or Coptic, which had been the language spoken by the priests and people of the region; the third was classic Greek. A French scholar, Jean-François Champollion—who knew both classic and demotic Greek—was able by comparing them to see they declared the same thing. Under the assumption that the third set of seeming-incomprehensible symbols was repeating the repeated text, he was able to decode it in 1822.

Think of the moment that multilingual Frenchman knew what he was looking at and first understood the stone. It had been more than twenty years since Napoleon's expedition to Egypt had brought back the recovered object, more than two thousand years since the scribe or scribes incised it with Ptolemy's decree. From that moment of discovery and comparative analysis, the history of Egypt and its written discourse opened out like a closed flower or a folded fan. Through an illustrative set of marks, it told the reader-scholar more than he otherwise could comprehend about the vanished past. Now the Rosetta Stone stands in much-visited glory in the British Museum in London. The language has lasted, will last.

Were we to draw the scene as cartoon, there would have been a light bulb igniting above Champollion's bent head; were his name Archimedes, we would have him exclaim "Eureka" while lolling in the bath. That sudden flash of inspiration, that moment when the world makes sense, is what we all experience when we first view written language and learn how to read. Without it we stare uncomprehending at serried marks on rock.

My argument therefore boils down to this: written discourse is a marker—both in the present moment and of the past and for the future—of what we hold most dear. Thought and emotions are inexpressible until by language expressed. Further, it's difficult to say a clear thing confusedly, or a confused thing clearly (unless, perhaps, I've managed to do so here). This is all the more true of writing, and it's why writing matters; a thing worth saying is worth transcribing well. *Writing matters. Why?* This is not a rhetorical question, but one that still needs to be asked.

a note on sources

As I stated at book's start, this is not a scholarly text. Most of the quotations here—from Yeats and Shakespeare et al.—are readily available if not already familiar to the interested reader. When I use a phrase from the Bible or Dante Alighieri, I trust—from my ascription on the page as such—that the source is clear. The citations that follow are more by way of explanatory notes than a full-fledged acknowledgment of the original passage, and the chapter by chapter referents are few and far between.

In Chapter 1, for instance, the only actual quotations come from the novel by Baroness Orczy and the poem by William Alfred, both situated on the page itself. When I declare my recollections of John Updike, John Gardner, and James Baldwin have been previously published, I cite—in the course of the chapter—their original venue and year.

But let me give slightly more detail. The portrait of John Updike was first composed for an autobiographical essay in 1985, and the version I here reproduce was published after his death in

John Updike Remembered, ed. Jack A. De Bellis (Jefferson, NC: McFarland & Company, 2017). The portrait of John Gardner comes from my Editor's Introduction to the posthumously published *Stillness and Shadows: Two Novels by John Gardner* (New York: Alfred A. Knopf, 1986), the passage on James Baldwin from *Running in Place: Scenes from the South of France* (New York: Atlantic Monthly Press, 1989).

Chapter 2 contains, to start with, both a paraphrase and précis of my Introduction to *The Sincerest Form: Writing Fiction by Imitation,* a textbook I published with McGraw-Hill in 2003. *Why Writing Matters* is—for its author, at least—the result of a lifelong commitment to writing and the teaching of writing, and I won't pretend I've never made these claims before. In no case are the passages verbatim, since I've cut and pasted and reconfigured language, but the argument itself has not been changed. By the time we move to the stichomythic dialogues, "the quick brown fox" and the discussion of Peter de Vries, the sentences are new.

Chapter 3 does quote from and rely on the published work of others. The passage on *The Communist Manifesto* has information provided by, and quotations from, *The Marx-Engels Reader,* ed. Robert C. Tucker (New York: W. W. Norton, 1978). The data as to dissemination of Harriet Beecher Stowe's work come from David S. Reynolds's *Mightier Than the Sword: Uncle Tom's Cabin and the Battle for America* (New York: W. W. Norton, 2011). Much of the discussion of Ms. Stowe's novel derives from my brother Andrew Delbanco's *The War before the War: Fugitive Slaves and the Struggle for America's Soul from the Revolution to the Civil War* (New York: Penguin, 2018). Chapter 3's third text is Darwin's, and the edition I use is *On the Origin of Species, by Means of Natural Selection* (1859; New York: Heritage Press, 1963). All quotations from Charles Darwin and his grandson are from this edition of the book. The text of "J'Accuse" is reprinted from the Paris newspaper *L'Aurore,* January 13, 1898, and the translation is mine. Finally, the edition of D. H. Lawrence's *Lady Chatterley's Lover* from which I quote is that of the University of Cambridge Press (2003).

Chapter 4 is shot through with citations, but they are each identified. Whether I reproduce the plaque on the site where Thomas Chatterton died, or the epigraph to *The Great Gatsby,* I do so, I believe, with sufficient specificity and in the realm of fair use. Chapter 5 ("Strategies in Prose") reprints briefly the work of five students—Dean Bakopolous, Michael Byers, Paisley Rekdal, Jess Row, and Leah Stewart (all of them now accomplished authors)—from a pamphlet we published together at the University of Michigan. They have granted permission to reprint their youthful efforts from that course in 1995, and I am very grateful. Grateful, as well, for my daughter Francesca Delbanco's participation and letter in Chapter 6.

That chapter, titled "Originality," includes sustained quotations from John Donne, Virginia Woolf, and William Blake. The first two are self-evident, but the quotations from Blake are drawn from *William Blake: The Complete Illuminated Books* (New York: Thames & Hudson, in association with the William Blake Trust, 2000). Near the end of Chapter 6, I reproduce passages from Alberto Manguel's excellent *A History of Reading,* and I want to urge that book on the reader's close attention. It provides a detailed accounting of its titular subject, and I have profited greatly from its author's insights. Chapter 6 also includes a line from Sarah Blakewell's *How to Live, or A Life of Montaigne in One Question and Twenty Attempts at an Answer* (New York: Other Press, 2010).

Chapter 7 begins with an additional quotation from Manguel; I am grateful for permission to reprint. (Excerpts from *A History of Reading* by Alberto Manguel, copyright © 1996 by Alberto Manguel. Used by permission of Viking Books, an imprint of Penguin Publishing Group, a division of Penguin Random House LLC. All rights reserved.) Further, it includes a passage from Henry David Thoreau's *Walden, or Life in the Woods,* as reproduced by the Library of America in 2009. The work by Bulwer-Lytton and Amanda McKittrick Ros is located in the text itself, and I want to repeat my gratitude to James Landis for his compilation both of the garbled newspaper headlines and writerly bon mots. The description of a display at the Morgan Library & Museum in New York is an eyewitness account, but that exhibition has since been catalogued and published as *The Magic of Handwriting: The Pedro Corrêa do Lago Collection* (Cologne: Taschen, 2018).

Chapter 8 contains a letter from Mary Shelley included in that catalogue, as well as material obtained from the Chamber of Commerce's description of Saranac, New York. Chapters 8 and 9 (with the brief exception of lines from Yeats, Woolf, Auden, and Shakespeare) have only my own language. My colleague George Bornstein, an expert on the poet's work, pointed me to Yeats's revisions in the drafts of "Adam's Curse." Throughout this final stage of production I've profited from the close supervisory expertise of Dan Heaton and of Julie Carlson, whose copy-editing has been excellence itself: all thanks. The Postscript does include citations from two studies of national literacy: https://www.nationsreportcard.gov and https://nces.ed.gov/naal/kf_demographics.asp. But I want to end where I began: with the assertion that a book like this is shot through with quotation and inescapably allusive; to footnote every reference would be to double its length.

Nicholas Delbanco is the author of more than thirty works of fiction and non-fiction. His most recent publications are the novel *The Years*, and essay collection *Curiouser and Curiouser*. Among the ten books he has edited are *The Sincerest Form* and *Literature: Craft and Voice*. Delbanco co-founded the Bennington Writing Workshops, ran the University of Michigan's Helen Zell Writers' Program, and directed the Hopwood Awards Program. He served as judge for numerous writing prizes, including the Pen/Faulkner Prize in Fiction and the Pulitzer Prize in Fiction, and chaired the National Book Awards in Fiction. Among his own awards are the J. S. Guggenheim Memorial Fellowship and, twice, the National Endowment for the Arts Fellowship in prose fiction. Fifty years ago, the *New York Times* declared, of Delbanco, "An excellent writer is among us . . . and if we neglect him, we shall have to apologize to posterity." The *Chicago Tribune* called him "As fine a pure prose stylist as any writer living," and this book too merits that praise.

Featuring intriguing pairings of authors and subject, each volume in the Why X Matters series presents a concise argument for the continuing relevance of an important idea.

Also in the series